ISBN
1
8566
9
224
8

laurence king

published in 2000 by
laurence king publishing
an imprint of
calmann & king ltd
71 great russell street
london wc1b 3bn
t +44 20 7831 6351
f +44 20 7831 8356
e enquiries@calmann-
king.co.uk
www.laurence-king.com

copyright & text &
design 2000 Intro

a catalogue record for
this book is available
from the british library

ISBN 1 85669 224 8

printed in hong kong

Searching for the authentic

Adrian Shaughnessy

The range of graphic expression and stylistic hybridity found within contemporary music graphics barely qualifies for the term 'graphic design'. Of course, we are not talking about the CD covers that fill up the racks in chain stores and high-street multiples. Rather, we are talking about the sleeves for 'other musics' – what the mainstream record industry lazily lumps together and calls 'alternative music'. In other words, music released by underground labels run by single-minded visionaries; music from obscure labels catering for hyper-rarefied tastes; music with sales figures that would scarcely fund the upkeep of a hamster. You can spot these records a mile off. They often don't have barcodes and they nearly always have arty covers, or at least covers that make you look twice.

When we look at radical album covers from the past few years, we recognize many of the formal attributes of graphic design – typography, layout, illustration and the use of familiar printing techniques – but we see other things that seem alien to the conventions of graphic design, closer in fact to modern art. We see stylistic contortions that plunge us into the unconscious world of dreams and nocturnal imaginings; we see semiotic daubings and scratchings; we see impenetrable, un-readable text (coded typography for initiates only),[1] we see imagery that is sometimes brutal and ugly, sometimes limpid and beautiful. But is it graphic design?

Clearly, we are not in the familiar, everyday world of instantaneous consumer gratification. We have turned our back on slick one-size-fits-all graphic design. We have left the world of can't-fail marketing strategies. The 'legible' has given way to the 'illegible', the 'easy' has succumbed to the 'difficult', the 'commercial' has become the 'un-commercial'. But is it art?

The proposition, 'Can graphic design ever be art?' has preoccupied thinking designers and commentators since the start of design as a formal discipline. Is it conceivable that the design of a magazine, a newspaper, a logo, a book jacket, might qualify as art? Who in their right mind would describe, for example, the graphics on a tube of toothpaste as art? But what about a record cover that disregards the conventions of consumerism, that does not even have the musician's name on the front cover, and relies solely on the emotive impact of poetic imagery and cryptic allusion? Many of the sleeves contained in this book (and its predecessor *Sampler: Contemporary Music Graphics*) fit this category. But are they art or graphic design? In order to decide, it is necessary to scrutinize the current state of graphic design and to look at the conflicting sensibilities that drive this all-pervading and enveloping mode of visual communication.

Often seen by outsiders as a homogeneous discipline, the contemporary practice of graphics is, one might argue, split between two camps. In the first camp, we find those who see it as one of the key constituents of modern business strategy: put simply, adherents to this pragmatic view of design – we'll call them the Pragmatists – believe that design is a marketing tool, just another weapon in the armoury of companies fighting the pitched battles of modern commerce. This view finds its strongest expression in the big international design groups, and in the boardrooms, marketing teams and corporate communications departments of the large companies who are the principal purchasers of graphic design skills and services. The other camp – a much smaller grouping – believes that graphic design is more than a strategic business resource. For them, design is no longer an invisible craft circumscribed by the conventions of typography, layout and printing technology. Instead, through its omnipresence in the modern world, it has come to occupy an increasingly significant position in the cultural life of a media-savvy population, and has achieved a degree of recognition unthinkable in previous decades. Adherents to this view may be described as the design-as-culture school: let's call them the Romantics.

Of course, graphic design cannot be divided as simplistically as this. Its practice in the 21st century subdivides into numerous categories. Information design, for example, occupies a supremely practical position in the world of visual communication – choose the wrong typeface for a highway intersection sign and you might kill someone. More rarefied kinds of design include interface design, font design, broadcast graphics and the many different kinds of technical graphics – from complex graphs to how-to-do-it instruction guides. Nevertheless, it can be said that, intellectually and emotionally, modern designers tend to fall into one or other of the two camps described.

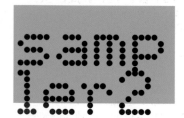

If we examine the rival claims of both camps, we find that the split is a familiar one – a kind of Roundheads and Cavaliers schism for the digital age. The first thing to note about the Pragmatists is that they hardly even want to be designers. It's almost as if the big design groups are embarrassed to be associated with design, as if it comes too low down the consultancy food chain. They sense that the real hard core action – the big fees, the kill-or-be-killed thrill of the chase – happens elsewhere. They look enviously at the income generated by management consultants, advertising agencies and e-commerce strategists, and they see design, with its sweat-of-the-brow connotations of manual labour and craft, as no longer part of the high-powered business world. Gradually design is replaced by the modern black arts of brand stewardship, corporate image management, design strategy and a dozen other corporate support mechanisms straight out of the business school manual.

On the other hand, the Romantic view of graphic design is that it is art, or at least aspires to the nature of art. This aesthetics-first stance frequently brings the Romantics into conflict with the ever-cautious forces of commerce and the design establishment. Another defining characteristic of the Romantic tendency is its belief in the value of self-expression. Often misinterpreted as self-interest, it is, in its higher manifestations, a search for unformulaic expression, a quest for original work and a rejection of the notion of the designer as passive, neutral and voiceless. In an interview, the New York-based designer Stefan Sagmeister (pages 78-81) described how he planned to close his studio for a 'year without clients' and work on his own projects.[2] It is this need for self-expression that most clearly differentiates the two camps.

The Romantic faction is further characterized by an unwillingness to accept the role of the graphic designer as unquestioning servant of the modern consumerist society. In the past this unease was expressed politically; there is a long tradition stretching back to William Morris, of designers allying themselves to political radicalism. Today this discomfort usually manifests itself in the creation of 'un-commercial' design statements such as 'difficult' typography and 'allusive' imagery. This introspective approach is often justified by its perpetrators as 'design that makes the viewer work', a concept often at odds with commercial interests and one which can result in the designer's equivalent of the death penalty – summary rejection.

However, even if we accept the Pragmatic/Romantic model of contemporary design practice, neither side can be said to have a monopoly on virtue. The Pragmatists are well-intentioned individuals, striving to make a living in an increasingly brutal and competitive world. They provide employment for many thousands of people, either directly or in ancillary services like printing, and they help many businesses and organizations grow and prosper. As W A Dwiggins, creator of the term 'graphic design', noted in 1922, 'When placards are put up at the corner garage announcing the current price of gasoline, they do not need to be fine art.'[3]

Yet this schism remains at the very heart of the debate about the nature of contemporary graphic design. If we fail to recognize this fundamental dichotomy, we are more likely to accept the dominant view that design is simply a business tool – a neutral voice for communication only – and that there is no place for notions of art and self-expression in what is arguably the most pervasive mode of visual communication. But the Pragmatists are choosing an odd moment to make public their disengagement with the design process. By doing so now, they run the risk of being wrong-footed by deep-running trends in the cultural landscape. There is strong evidence to suggest that the entire terrain of visual communication is changing, and that perhaps there *is* a place for graphic design-as-art. As the writer Will Self noted, when summarizing the 1990s: 'Food, design and other even more tenuous crafts have come to supersede the genuine arts as the repository of cultural aspiration.' It is clear from his use of the words 'tenuous' and 'genuine' that Self intends no compliment to design, but it is also obvious that he sees design as occupying a central (if to him unwelcome) role in the cultural life of contemporary society.[4]

The writer Angela McRobbie expresses a similar view, but without Self's haughty disdain, in her book *In the Culture Society* (Routledge, 1999). In McRobbie's opinion, we are living in the 'culture society', where culturally based activities such as television, film, music, fashion, art, leisure and entertainment now form a substantial part of the real-world economy – the world of work, careers and mortgages. In her perceptive and absorbing study, she examines the rise of the 'culture industries' in the UK and the importance placed upon them by the country's current Labour government. She refers to research which suggests that, 'culture now fires the engine of economic growth', and she coins the phrase 'the aestheticisation of everyday life' to explain the notion of a society where value is placed on cultural expression and aesthetic innovation. Her argument is based on an examination of the financial and cultural importance of music, fashion and art, but her ideas extend into all aspects of the everyday world, and one could argue that there is nothing more 'everyday' than graphic design.

Perhaps graphic designers have reached a point where it is possible to exist in the 'real world' (a favourite phrase of the Pragmatists) and earn a living producing work that is expressive and iconoclastic, but which does not end up in the box marked 'rejected'. Perhaps we have moved on from the formulaic and sanitized design 'solution' (another word popular with traditionalists) and into a period where aesthetic expression is valued for its ability to move the viewer? Perhaps we have entered a period where the design for products and services is genuinely 'distinguishable' ('differentiation' is the battle cry of the Pragmatists, but in reality sameness is prized above all other attributes); a period where the dubious sciences of branding and brand management are exposed as almost valueless in a volatile market-place where consumer intelligence is at its most powerful and where the internet, with its revolutionary new models of commerce, threatens to reduce cherished notions of brand identity to rubble.[5]

Advertising, in its most sophisticated forms, seems to live comfortably with the notions of self-expression and free-wheeling eclecticism. Star directors are brought in to shoot TV commercials that resemble mini-feature films and are encouraged to retain their trademark style. Scripts are written that resound with wit and knowing cultural references, and gently nudge us towards products and services in a tangential manner. As a consequence, the distinction between modern art and advertising appears less and less perceptible, and while much advertising remains crass and unimaginative, there is enough resonant and startling work smeared across billboards and on television to make us realize that some things have changed, and that perhaps McRobbie's notion of the 'aestheticisation of everyday life' has entered the souls of blue-chip advertisers and their agencies.

when i first began making
films . . . my starting
point was music . . .
i can remember loads
of record sleeves; the
ones i liked best were
the ones that featured
pictures of the groups,
standing together in
some arrangement . . .
what was on the covers,
with the kinks for
instance, corresponded
to my idea of cinema:
filming people head on,
with a fixed camera,
and keeping a
certain distance.

wim wenders

'le souffle de l'ange' in
the logic of images
faber and faber

So, to be aligned with the Romantic view of graphic design is no longer to be part of a misfit tendency, feeding off scraps and working on second-rate projects for marginal industries. Indeed, it may be argued that in a society where everything has a monetary value, and where, after television and film, graphic design might legitimately claim to be the dominant visual force of our time, there may now be a 'business' value in work that possesses an emotional force which extends beyond the strict parameters of traditional graphic design. And with 'Sensation', Brit art and the Saatchi Collection, a time when the definition of art is at its most elastic, and when the discourse surrounding the distinction between high and low is at its most active, it should be possible to include *some* graphic design in this definition of art. Certainly, if we think of art as including that which the art critic Mathew Collings calls 'very modern art' – he's referring to the work of Tracey Emin, Damien Hirst and Gary Hume – then it seems extremely easy to take advantage of the term's elasticity and admit large chunks of graphic design. But where do we find suitable candidates? We've already discounted the Pragmatic view of design, and staked the claim of designers from the Romantic school. And there is no more congenial a home for the Romantic sensibility than design for music, which, despite the 'Fast Moving Consumer Goods' mentality currently displayed by the major labels, still provides an outlet for graphic experimentation and unfettered expression.

This book's predecessor, *Sampler: Contemporary Music Graphics*, investigated the record industry's attitude towards sleeve design. It looked at the effect of the convergence of label ownership as the major labels mopped up all the smaller ones. It looked at the fall-out caused by changes in music retailing. It examined the effect on music-industry designers of miniaturization, as sleeves shrunk to fit the compact disc and the newer mini disc format, and it also looked at the evolution of the music video, and speculated on the likely effect of the internet. In the short time since the book was first published (Spring 1999), the decline of graphic design's importance within the mainstream music industry has accelerated. As a record company executive said to me recently – before defecting to the world of online music – 'Sleeves are not important in the new scheme of things. They don't figure in the equation any longer. The major labels revolve round the needs of the promotion department. The sleeve is an irrelevancy when it comes to the rush to service records to press, radio and television.'

Looking at the great mass of records that fill the release schedules of the modern music business, it might appear that sleeve design is no longer an activity worthy of serious attention. We find an ocean of tiny squares filled with impoverished graphics, anodyne photographs and vacuous imagery. Nothing indicates more dramatically the creative stagnation of the mainstream record industry than the state of the record cover. Once a vehicle for artistic expression that attracted the best minds in design, photography and art direction, it is now an endangered species, forced out into the chilly margins of an industry unsure about its future in a sector where the internet looms menacingly. If sleeve design is to survive, it is dependent on a triumvirate of bodies remaining committed to the notion of record-sleeves-as-art. The first of these bodies are the small independent record labels. The second are designers unconcerned with remuneration and mainstream professional recognition. And the third are maverick musicians who reject the received industry wisdom that states that a photograph of the artist is right for every cover.[6]

In a review of *Sampler*, design writer Rick Poynor pointed out that, 'No one minds when Jack Kerouac's *On The Road* gets a new cover design. Woe betide the marketing genius who one day decides that *Sergeant Pepper* needs a graphic makeover.'[7] This comment illustrates the enduring qualities of the best sleeve design and emphasizes the symbiotic relationship between music and cover. Furthermore, it reminds us that record sleeves from previous eras were designed without the benefit of focus groups and formulaic marketing strategies, and that the best sleeve design is usually a powerful statement of graphic individualism. Record covers, at their best, are inseparable from the rich personal experience and enjoyment of the music itself. In an interview, the musician Tim Gane of Stereolab explained his own vision of the relationship between music and sleeve: 'Music is only 50% at most, we always say we make music for records; it isn't complete, or doesn't properly exist until it's on the record and becomes an object, a thing… Then you have the design elements, even down to the colour of the vinyl, and this becomes a part of the sound. You have an image whether you like it or not, even if it's a non-image. The visual presentation of the record as artefact is a way in which we deal with the problem of image. It takes the attention off us as individuals. This is a very non-rock thing to do and the music press can't deal with things on this level.'[8] It's this deep-rooted connection between a record and its cover that makes sleeve design such a fertile subject for investigation.

Over the past few decades, record covers have been fetishized and adopted as tribal and subcultural emblems. At their best, they represent a peak of creative expression within graphic design. But perhaps the terminology surrounding sleeve design is unhelpful. Within the record industry, music is referred to as 'product' and sleeves are described as 'packaging'. Yet it's hardly 'packaging' in the accepted sense of the term. Design awards catering for the graphic design community, for instance, rarely include record covers in their packaging sections. If they include them at all, it is usually in a special 'music' section. It's as if record sleeves lack the disposability characteristic of nearly all packaging. They are clearly *not* viewed in the same way as perfume boxes, breakfast cereal cartons or frozen pea packets; and this is understandable because record sleeves *are* different: unlike nearly all other types of packaging, they are not thrown away. Instead, they are kept, often treasured and venerated. And since sleeves can affect our response to the music, our appreciation amplified by the degree to which we engage with the cover, the argument that we keep record covers merely to 'protect' discs (vinyl particularly) is of no consequence to the serious music lover. Record sleeves are part of the music and part of the experience of 'reading' the sound. At their most compelling, they guide us to a greater understanding of the music they envelope.

However, this is not how today's major labels see it. When they commission record sleeves, their sole intention is to create highly tailored design that will influence our decision to purchase. Understandable though this may be, the outcome tends to be bland uniformity. Certainly *Sergeant Pepper*, possibly the most celebrated record cover ever and frequently used to further the cause of radical sleeve design, cannot be included in the list of record company commissioned sleeves. The Beatles commissioned it themselves (with the help of art dealer Robert Fraser), and the imagination quails at the thought of what it might have looked like if the EMI publicity department had, as was normal at the time, been responsible for the design. As Tim Gane's comments make clear, the most successful covers are those that employ the musician in a curatorial role. This happens in one of the following ways: the musician finds an image that has a certain resonance for him or her; the musician commissions a designer/artist who shares his or her aesthetic sensibility; the musician designs his or her own cover. But the intention is the same: to make a seamless production, a unified creative statement – music and image as one.

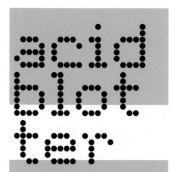

acid
blot
ter

the cover - a simulation
of a perforated sheet
of acid blotters - is
so convincing that a
young man in texas,
pulled over for a
traffic violation, was
arrested when the cops
saw the cd insert lying
on his car seat. 'he
was thrown in jail for
a couple of days while
the cops tested it'
says hawtin, 'i felt
sorry for the kid but
i don't know if he was
showing off to his
friends, pretending he
had acid. there were
people who ate the
whole thing, trying to
get a buzz off it.

simon reynolds

writing about sheet
one, the 1993 debut cd
from plastikman (richie
hawtin), in his book
energy flash
picador

Some reviewers of the first *Sampler* confessed to being mystified by many of the sleeves reproduced in that book, and asked for greater explication. Of course, in order to create an alluring cover, and to encourage further exploration, a sense of mystery has been a feature of many of the best sleeves from the past 30 years. Nevertheless, it is worth looking at a few of the dominant trends in current sleeve design, if only to identify themes and patterns that will resurface later in mainstream visual communication.

Perhaps the most noticeable tendency is the one the writer and critic Michael Bracewell identified in a book review: 'Throughout the 1990s, a common theme of new trends was the quest for authenticity…'[9] Bracewell's remark is apt in the context of sleeve design. Authenticity in graphic expression is demonstrably one of the defining characteristics of many recent sleeves and a recurring element in much of the work contained in this book. It manifests itself in various forms, although it can be seen principally in a return to illustration, painting and old-fashioned mark-making. It is plainly a reaction to the high degree of image fabrication and manipulation found in the mainstream music industry, and indeed in visual communication as a whole. The trend has its origins in the record covers of American post-rock and lo-fi bands, who have harnessed the vernacular power of simple, and sometimes frankly crude, imagery. It is undoubtedly anti-design, just as it is anti-corporate and anti-music business. And while some design commentators see this as an apparent 'dumbing-down' process, when viewed in tandem with developments in musical forms, this design trend can be seen as part of a serious attempt to resist the commodification of music, and displace hype and synthetic emotion. In its most successful manifestations, the authentic in sleeve design acquires a power and resonance beyond the reach of work exhibiting higher levels of graphic refinement.

Bound up with the notion of authenticity is the arrival over the past decade or so of musical forms that eschew the cult of pop celebrity. Here again, sleeve designers have been forced to look beyond the conventions of 'high-concept' graphic design. It's a bit like rock music itself: it's all been done already, and those bands who still trade in the redundant thump of the 4-square-rock-beat-with-guitars format, are seen as mere copyists or recyclers of rock's golden past. In graphic design, similar notions apply. Yet again, the path has been laid by young American slacker-generation bands, but also by dance music, with its anonymous high priest, the DJ (although the DJ as superstar is now an established paradigm), and its armies of anonymous producers, re-mixers and 'turntablists'. These, and a dozen other new musical genres, require sleeves with a different visual syntax. The ubiquitous artist picture is rarely an option. Instead, designers are forced to create imagery that captures the emotional power of the music and conveys an appropriate message to the intended audience. The ability to keep up with the thousands of records released each month is beyond all but the most dedicated aficionado. Names change and shift; production teams appear under different pseudonyms; artists hop from label to label. The only way to keep up is to learn to 'read' the sleeves; use them as maps through the undergrowth. And so sleeve designers become map-makers rather than image-makers: Greil Marcus used the memorable phrase 'three-minute utopias' to describe pop songs; he might have added that the best record covers form the cartography of these utopias.

As well as a yearning for authenticity, the recent increase in the number of covers featuring raw and untutored scribblings and scratchings (pages 76-77, 115) can also be attributed to a rejection of the computer by many designers as the central tool of graphic design execution. This can be seen as a reaction to the sterility of template-based design which has led to a drab uniformity throughout much graphic design. The DTP revolution is complete. Anyone can do it, and everyone does it. For the brave and the adventurous, the only option is to reject the tyranny of the grey box (they've become a bit more colourful recently, but they're still grey boxes!). And so we see the re-emergence of the colour pencil (Laurent Garnier, *Unreasonable Behaviour*, pages 120-121), the inky pen (Tim Berne, *Blood Count Discretion*, page 109) and the scissors and glue pot of the collagist (Fennesz, O'Rourke, Rehberg, *The Magic Sound of Fenno'berg*, pages 22-23).

sun ra

by hand printing the
covers, they could
avoid printing costs
altogether. often the
covers carried only a
simple title, or only
the location of the
recording in black ink;
but at times became
more elaborate, with
multicoloured grids,
rainbows, or astral
scenes; or there might
be photos of sun ra
pasted on, hand-tinted,
the whole cover
laminated with a piece
of textured plastic
shower curtain.
sometimes every cover
of a single record was
different.

john f. szwed

space is the place
the life and times of
sun ra
payback press

But the computer has not entirely departed from the radical sleeve design arena. Computer illustration, normally associated with computer games and the tackier end of dance music, is occasionally deployed with subtlety and gentle mockery in contemporary sleeve design. A striking example of this are the computer illustrations for the Mouse on Mars cover *Niun Niggung* (pages 138-139). A sophisticated assemblage of unexpected imagery, the cover alludes to the electronic montage sound of this influential German band. Their music is a distinctive melding of layers of gurgling electronic sound, real instruments and snatched samples, and this hybridity is carried into the sleeve art which features an orange monkey – hardly a typical image even in the world of album covers – cavorting over a shifting background of 'found' comic book art. Described by one commentator as if 'Terry Gilliam had been let loose on Photoshop…',[10] the sleeve design is in fact the work of the German design group Icon. The Cologne-based team have also created an alternative American version of *Niun Niggung* (page 92). This version features a blobby 3D comb and hairbrush. Reminiscent of the work of the late P Scott Makela, it has a twisted potency entirely in keeping with the music.

The modern independent record industry is no longer dominated by British and American record labels. The German independent label scene is a beacon of innovation and creativity in the current musical landscape. Reminiscent of the 'Kraut rock' era of the 1970s, when Germany last exerted a defining influence on contemporary music, the current German independent sector is thronged with radical labels and innovative bands, and appears uncontaminated by the inertia that pervades the British and American mainstream record industry. Companies like Kitty Yo, City Slang, Raster Noton, Mego (pages 22-23), Supposé (pages 46-47) and Source Records (pages 126-127) offer a radical template for the way labels can face the future. Their readiness to embrace new musical and graphical languages puts them firmly in the tradition of those visionary British and American labels that created the modern record industry. Their inventiveness and exuberance is confidently articulated in their sleeve design.

A different sort of radicalism is found in France. Although the French are notoriously inward-looking and confident in their innate Gallic-ness, it has been a characteristic of French culture throughout the modern era to absorb external artistic influences, and yet at the same time, remain quintessentially French. Debussy did it with Gamelan, and Ravel with the syncopations of jazz. Today, a new generation of French bands graft subtle influences on to unmistakably French modes of pop expression. A similar force is at work amongst sleeve designers. The sleeve for Mellow's *Instant Love* (pages 94-95) by Laurent Fetis, evokes thoughts of Peter Max and Alan Jones, and his sleeve for Tahiti 80 (page 41) assimilates Japanese comic art, yet both sleeves remain palpably French.

Isolated pockets of radicalism exist in other European countries, though few exhibit the visual lucidity of the Norwegian electronic-music label Rune Grammofon (pages 58-69). In its single-minded pursuit of its own idio-syncratic vision, the label resembles ECM, Manfred Eicher's venerable German company. Like those of the Munich-based ECM, Rune Grammofon sleeves are instantly identifiable, while the music retains a similarly distinctive footprint. Yet again, as with ECM, Rune Grammofon sleeves seem unaffected by design trends and fashionable stylistic reflexes. The sleeves, all by designer Kim Hiorthøy, have a refined elegance and a tactile sensuousness that comes partly from their confident execution, partly from their use of expressionistic illustration, and partly from their refusal to use conventional packaging. The label is publicly committed to cardboard packaging and rejects the ubiquitous Perspex 'jewel case' with its unyielding sense of permanence. As label founder Rune Kristoffersen states: '…we modestly aim to recapture the magic connected to the discovery of new artists and buying their records'.[11] As if to give flesh to the symbiotic link with Eicher's label, the Norwegian company is now distributed by ECM: Manfred Eicher's patronage imbues the label with an added glamour; the glamour of the authentic.

Further south in Milan, the Italian label Alga Marghen (pages 112-113) describes itself as documenting 'relevant contemporary sound research, representing some of the highest peaks in the radicalisation of sound musical languages'. This lofty ambition is mirrored in the label's sleeves: like academic notebooks these covers evoke the austere world of acoustical research and lifetimes spent studying the hidden laws of sound. Resembling the scholarly recordings of the 1960s they use period photographs and handwritten typography with unselfconscious ease, yet manage to look cool and superbly now-ish at the same time.

New thinking in typography has been one of the more lasting contributions made by sleeve design over the past few decades. A once invisible subject, typography has, like stand-up comedy, cooking and tantric sex, been hailed as the new rock and roll. Yet within current sleeve design, its role seems somewhat diminished. It now appears to be no more important than any other aspect of the design lexis. Of course, there are exceptions: the CD cover for Pauline Oliveros' *at the ijsbreker jan 21, 1999* (pages 48-49), is a typography-only design. This unmistakably Dutch sleeve appears, within the context of contemporary sleeve design, both eccentric and studious. In a world of cyber letterforms and Carson-like grunge, this sleeve's Spartan simplicity and lack of shrillness is a welcome diversion.

Elsewhere in these pages, typography skitters about stylistically, seemingly avoiding the straightjacket of fashion. We find less of the modish Swiss-school modernism, fashionable amongst British record-cover designers over the past decade or so, and a greater use of typographic diversity and uncategorizable innovation. The work of my Intro colleague Mat Cook is revealing in this context. He pursues a disciplined typographic path – which he marries up to high-end art direction. Cook, like Farrow (pages 42-45), Blue Source (pages 54-57) and Designers Republic (pages 20-21, 32-33, 88-89, 106-107, 133), underpins most of his work with the coolly restrained typography of Swiss high-modernism, but his series of sleeves for Archive (pages 14-17) utilizes the typographic styling of official forms and government questionnaires. Cook's typography for Archive, when linked to his assiduously art-directed photography, conveys a fashionable sense of post-modern alienation, entirely appropriate to the keyboard-driven sound-scapes of the band's music. With most of the sleeves featured in these pages, 'eclectic' seems to be the new watchword in record sleeve typography.

Eclecticism is certainly a feature of the work of Trevor Jackson. A musician, designer and record-label owner, Jackson represents an intriguing twist to the definition of sleeve designer – the sleeve designer-as-musician-as-label-owner. On the surface, it looks as if he has been given the keys to the candy store, but Jackson's three roles require reservoirs of courage and ingenuity beyond the capabilities of many graphic designers. His work is resolutely un-commercial: most of his sleeves would induce apoplexy in the marketing departments of the major labels. But for a small band of devotees, Jackson's work represents a siren call of radicalism and the true iconoclastic spirit of sleeve design. His sleeve for Icarus (pages 96-97) contains

its own wry comment on the unyielding nature of the record business. As with most labels, Output is occasionally subjected to the ignominy of 'returns'. (A much-loathed aspect of the life of a small label, 'returns' are unsold records returned by retailers with the consequent loss of revenue to the label.) As if this was not punishment enough, the covers invariably come back damaged, thus preventing their resale. Jackson's 'situationist' response to this is to fabricate 'damaged' covers at the outset, and encourage additional wear and tear from the record-buying public and careless distributors. He gives a new twist to the notion of 'buying damaged goods'.

The hand-made aesthetics of Jackson's Output label can also be seen in the work of Fat Cat Recordings (pages 98-99). The hand-drilled holes in the sleeves of the label's 'Split Series' are redolent of Josef Beuys' multiples. These sleeves thumb their noses at the inexorable process of commodification that characterizes the modern record industry as much as it does the world of consumer goods. So too does the 'cardboard box' of Hydrogen Dukebox's *Ripsnorter* (page 137). I discovered this delightful little package, with its recycled aesthetics and 'found' graphic motifs, in the unlikely locale of the Virgin Megastore in London's Oxford Street. The pleasure of finding this package, designed by British sleeve designers Yacht, was akin to the excitement of buying a piece of art: you imagine it's the only one.

With the work of Rudy VanderLans, we again find the draconian constraints of the modern record industry contributing to the forging, rather than the destruction of, a definable aesthetic for small labels. Better known as the editor of *Emigre* magazine, and the creator of fonts that helped redefine typography in the late 1980s and early 1990s, VanderLans uses his magazine to sell a small catalogue of recorded music via mail order. His box-with-feathers for Itchy Pet's *Dreaming out Louder* (page 132) is unthinkable within the context of modern record retailing, while his lavish book-with-CD *Palm Desert* (pages 50-53) is equally untypical and uncompromising in its refusal to conform to industry-accepted notions of how CDs should be packaged. VanderLans' photographs document his travels in *America deserta* and evoke south-west USA in a manner that makes you ache to be there. His restrained typography is a welcome respite from the experimental and dysfunctional typography of many sleeves.

When compared to VanderLans' work, the mid-west label Jade Tree represents an alternative reading of the American sleeve design scene. This small label produces sleeves with a paradoxically European flavour. The sleeve for the Joan of Arc album *Live in Chicago 1999* (pages 116-117) perhaps best exemplifies this. Photographed by Andy Mueller of design company Ohiogirl (he also designed the Isotope sleeves on pages 90-91), the band is depicted enacting scenes from Jean-Luc Godard's new-wave classic *Weekend*. The village hall 'am-dram' aesthetics give the sleeve a remote intellectual quality curiously at odds with the defiant anti-intellectualism of most sleeve design. And here we find another trait of radical sleeve design: an unwillingness to trade in the referential history of pop music. It's as if to acknowledge the iconography of rock and pop is to remain forever looking backwards, submerged in rock's heritage, at a time when whole areas of the contemporary music scene are as far removed from rock's triumphalist past as they are from ballroom dancing.

However, an intriguing example of 'looking backwards' is the cover for *Avant Hard* by Add N to (X) (pages 24-27). But this is no misty-eyed longing for rock's glorious past. Instead, it looks out over the world of audio research labs, and perhaps to Joe Meek in his makeshift recording studio in the Holloway Road where he created an analogue sound that ran through 1960s British pop like a dark undercurrent, and which can still be heard in hip hop and other fractured sound worlds. Designed by the band in collaboration with Mute's Paul Taylor, the sleeve functions as a visual manifesto for the music. It announces the band's influences and intentions, and the imagery drip-feeds their obsession with the fetishistic appeal of analogue recording hardware; a slogan on the cover confirms this interest: 'A new heart to analogue.' The non-digital spirit is further enforced by the use of Archigram-style gizmo architecture and the collagist aesthetics of Eduardo Paolozzi. It also recalls the assemblages of photographer Michael Cooper (*Sergeant Pepper's Lonely Hearts Club Band* and *Their Satanic Majesties Request,* both 1967). If *Avant Hard* had been released in 1967, it would have been hailed by sleeve enthusiasts as a classic of the genre. Instead, it slots effortlessly into the contemporary graphic landscape: a sleeve for those who look forward as well as backwards.

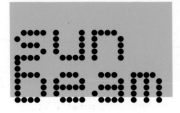

A more straightforwardly modern aesthetic sensibility is found in the sleeves of Ekhornforss. London-based designer Jon Forss and Norwegian photographer Kjell Ekhorn produce sleeves of enigmatic beauty with few discernible antecedents. Their sleeve for Cologne-based 'ultrafunk' practitioner Oliver Braun, who records under the pseudonym Beige (pages 72-73), has a dysfunctional beauty. Forss' 'Hoover bag' sleeve for Thurston Moore (page 136) is reminiscent of work found in an avant garde art gallery. Equally modern are Sheffield-based The Designers Republic. Best known for their recycling of the detritus of cyber-culture, in recent years they have shifted direction, and a new refinement seems to have entered their work. Gone are the data streams of faux-corporate logos and the evocation of a Blade Runner-like dystopia. Instead, their work reveals a greater sense of control and poise. Who would have guessed the design author-ship of their Peel Sessions series of sleeves (pages 106-107)? These austere covers hardly resemble typical DR sleeves. Nor is their work for Campag Velocet (pages 88-89), Phoenecia (pages 32-33) and Autechre (page 133) typical of their recent output. Most of their sleeves are produced for the Warp label, and surely this must qualify as one of the most exciting and fruitful unions between a label and a design house? As a body of work, it has surpassed many of the other great designer/record company partnerships of recent years. DR remains notoriously aloof from the competitive snake-pit of the modern record business. Founder Ian Anderson adopts an uncompromising attitude to record industry procedures surrounding the awarding of contracts to design companies, and individual designers. His disdain for the commercial hoop-jumping, often required to win the plum jobs, is commendable. He pursues a vision of the utmost singularity and intensity.

A similar insularity and detachment characterizes Primal Scream. My company, Intro, has worked with the band on the design of their two most recent albums. The paths taken to arrive at a cover design, and the ensuing repercussions, form an interesting case study and commentary on the contemporary sleeve-design process. Primal Scream are unquestionably popular, with substantial global record sales. But as a band, they remain wilfully uncompliant with record industry processes, and refuse to participate in many of the promotional activities that traditionally boost sales. The cover and campaign design for their current album Exterminator (pages 34-37), provides

a rich source of evidence for this intractability. Designed by Julian House (this book's designer and co-editor), the process began, as it had done previously, with the band playing House and I lengthy chunks of newly recorded music. Bobby Gillespie and Andrew Innes supply insights into the themes and components of the music, and gradually scenarios and fragments of ideas for covers emerge.

A new Primal Scream album is an important event in the life of Primal Scream fans. The band holds the view that their covers should be an event, and as avid record collectors themselves, they know the indefinable thrill of a great record wrapped in a great cover. In the case of Exterminator, we set out to create a cover that lived up to the ambition and raw grandeur of their music. Two events assisted in this process. The first was the near-total closure of the band's record label Creation, halfway through the life of the project. The second was the development by Julian House of a typographic treatment of their name, that dispensed with vowels. Primal Scream became 'Prml Scrm', and Exterminator became 'Xtrmntr'. Both names remain oddly comprehensible in much the way that abbreviations in road signs and the truncated text messages widely used in modern paging systems remain legible. This idea met with some resistance from Creation, but for Primal Scream it struck the right note of subversion and provocation. Concurrent with this, House prepared visuals infused with various themes played out in the band's lyrics. War has been a recurring theme in Primal Scream mythology and House used this as a source of imagery and developed an elaborate Pop Art vision of Gulf War iconography; jets, nuclear weapons and the hardware of modern warfare. He subverted these images, familiar from hundreds of TV news reports, by using the distortions of perspective and logic found in the work of Pop artists like Richard Hamilton. After frequent discussions with Bobby Gillespie and Andrew Innes, a coherent campaign emerged built around vowel-less typography, and a Pop Art version of the Gulf War (complete with Baudrillardian overtones!).[12]

An interesting by-product of this was the adoption of the vowel-less typography by the music press. Articles appeared for weeks after the release of the record, making humorous references to Primal Scream's disavowal of vowels. Style magazine The Face ran a story in its 20th Anniversary issue called

The End of the Vowel',[13] noting Primal Scream's prescience in this new linguistic trend. This simple typographic device generated enough media coverage for even the most ambitious record industry press officer, and its adoption by music journalists proved that album covers can still be events and need not be the pallid little blips on the cultural radar screens that most have become.

Yet if the album cover is to survive it will have to learn to live with the modern media meltdown. The internet offers the most serious threat to the record sleeve as music fans flock to websites where free music is available at the click of a mouse. Music is already migrating to the online world faster than the experts claim. Sites like www.napster.com are virtual record shops full of tracks from every well-known name in the pop firmament, waiting to be downloaded – for free. All you have to do is offer your own cache of MP3 treasure in exchange. It's a new world-economy; you pay nothing; everything is an exchange; you take twenty tracks, you give one in return. In America, campus internet servers wilt under the strain of continuous use, and the record companies pursue the miscreant sites through the courts. It's a tantalizing glimpse into a future world where entertainment is taken out of the hands of the 'cultural producers' and made available in a free-for-all global market of barter; a cyber-space version of the medieval market square where one Massive Attack track is swapped for three Sonic Youth tracks.[14]

But the world of dot.com music is visually unalluring. It's a 72dpi world of icy interfaces and invisible data streams. No colour. No humanity. No record covers: just grey buttons. If we are to lose the album cover, what will replace it in the affections of millions? What will supply us with such a diverse and eclectic mix of imagery and sheer visual oddness? Where will the Romantic designer go to let off steam? Where will visual culture turn to receive its regular blood transfusions of new ideas? Record covers are by no means the only place to find innovation and originality, but in a world where everything looks the same, the best album covers supply a myriad of tiny lenses through which it is sometimes possible to glimpse other worlds and other conditions.

columbia also began
some systematic image
building, projecting
miles davis as the
byronic black man, the
'mean, moody and
magnificent' jazz
musician. The cover of
the first cbs album,
round about midnight,
showed a brooding miles
in sepia tints, his eyes
masked with dark
glasses, his down
turned head in his
hands and his trumpet
slung across his chest.
the cover of milestones
was to have a
magnificent portrait of
him in open-necked
green shirt, sitting
down and staring
impassively at the
camera. years later,
this would inspire one
of joe zawinull's
compositions, 'the man
in the green shirt'.

ian carr

miles davis:
the definitive
biography
harper collins

Notes

1 I found the sleeve for HollAnd's single *Neoprene So Tight* (page 115) in the wonderful New York record shop, Other Music. The illegible Twombley-like handwriting and the tiny picture in the bottom left-hand corner immediately marked out the cover as prime *Sampler 2* material. Along with an armful of other treasure, I took it up to the sales counter, where each title was keyed into a computer by the sales assistant. When she came to the HollAnd sleeve, she looked worried. 'Who is this record by?' she asked. Sheepishly, I admitted that I didn't know. I felt eyebrows being raised in the queue behind me. What sort of jerk buys a record without knowing the name of the artist?

2 Interview with Stefan Sagmeister by Lynda Relph-Knight in *Design Week*, 3 March 2000.

3 'A New Kind of Printing Calls for New Design' by W A Dwiggins. Written in 1922 and reproduced in *Looking Closer 3*, edited by Michael Bierut, Jessica Helfand, Steven Heller and Rick Poynor (Allworth Press, 1999).

4 Interview with Will Self in *The Independent on Sunday*, 28 November 2000.

5 For a coruscating attack on big design group thinking, see Stephen Bayley's 'Hallelujah! Praise the Brands', *Blueprint* No. 169, February 2000.

6 For more on this subject, see 'Pop Goes the Easel' by Alice Rawsthorn in *Wallpaper** 145. The title of the article was first used for a BBC film on Pop Art made by Ken Russell and broadcast in February 1962.

7 Review of *Sampler: Contemporary Music Graphics* by Rick Poynor in *AIGA Journal*, Vol. 17, No. 2, 1999.

8 From a lengthy interview with Tim Gane of Stereolab by Robert Garnett in *e2:4 the creamy issue*, 1998.

9 From a review by Michael Bracewell of *Repetitive Beat Generation* by Steve Redhead (Rebel Inc., 2000) in *The Independent Weekend Review*, 4 March 2000.

10 Article on Mouse Orl Mars by Rob Young in *The Wire* No. 188, October 1999.

11 Found on the Rune Grammofon website, www.runegrammofon.com

12 Jean Baudrillard maintained that the 1991 Gulf War did not happen and was, in fact, a media fabrication. A recurring theme in conversations with Bobby Gillespie and Andrew Innes is their refusal to be informed by the news media and their inherent mistrust of official facts.

13 Uncredited article in *The Face* No. 40, May 2000.

14 Napster has created a sensation in the music press and the general media. Numerous articles recount the battles to suppress the site. For a comprehensive account of the turmoil surrounding Napster, see Steve Sutherland's article 'Game Over. Will Napster Destroy the Music Business?', *NME*, 10 June 2000.

norico.com

syn

norico.com

screen grabs of
interlacing images
designed for the web.
production of printed
material adheres to
the screen aesthetic-
all artwork produced
in pixels.

design: mason wells
at north
syn producrion
1999

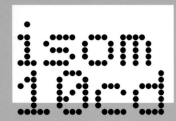

archive
take my head

cd booklet spreads
art direction & design:
mat cook @ intro
photography: rick guest
independiente
1999

▶ | Archive

Do not remove

Remove

01 Item or group? *Objet ou groupe?*	**04** Item or group? *Objet ou groupe?*
02 Item or group? *Objet ou groupe?*	**05** Item or group? *Objet ou groupe?*
03 Item or group? *Objet ou groupe?*	**06** Item or group? *Objet ou groupe?*
01 Item or group? *Objet ou groupe?*	**04** Item or group? *Objet ou groupe?*
02 Item or group? *Objet ou groupe?*	**05** Item or group? *Objet ou groupe?*
03 Item or group? *Objet ou groupe?*	**06** Item or group? *Objet ou groupe?*

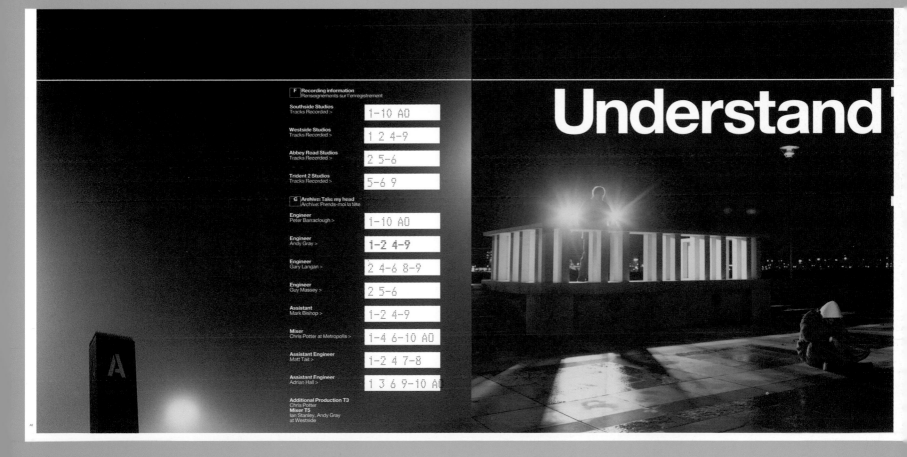

Understand T

F Recording information
Renseignements sur l'enregistrement

Southside Studios Tracks Recorded >	1-10 A0
Westside Studios Tracks Recorded >	1 2 4-9
Abbey Road Studios Tracks Recorded >	2 5-6
Trident 2 Studios Tracks Recorded >	5-6 9

G Archive: Take my head
Archive: Prends-moi la tête

Engineer Peter Barraclough >	1-10 A0
Engineer Andy Gray >	1-2 4-9
Engineer Gary Langan >	2 4-6 8-9
Engineer Guy Massey >	2 5-6
Assistant Mark Bishop >	1-2 4-9
Mixer Chris Potter at Metropolis >	1-4 6-10 A0
Assistant Engineer Matt Tait >	1-2 4 7-8
Assistant Engineer Adrian Hall >	1 3 6 9-10 A0

Additional Production T3
Chris Potter
Mixer T5
Ian Stanley, Andy Gray
at Westside

fsuk 2

the future sound of the
united kingdom two

cd booklet pages
illustration:
joel lardner
ministry of sound
recordings ltd
1998

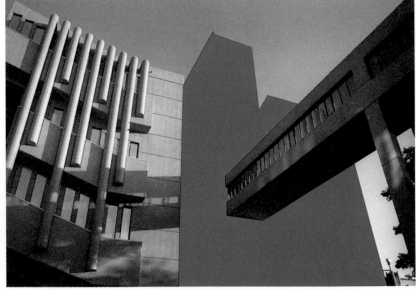

warp
029

warp10+1 influences

cd booklet spreads
design: the designers
republic
warp
1999

fennesz, o'rourke,
rehberg
the magic sound of
fenno'berg

cd front & inner details
artwork & photographic
representation of
fenno'berg: chicks on
speed
mego
1999

ALL tracks played by Christian Fennesz.
Jim O'Rourke & Peter Rehberg at:
ICC Tokyo 17 Jan '99 (1+6)
Some old raft floating in Hamburg Harbour 8 May '98
Die insel, BERLIN 5 May '98 (3)
RHIZ, VIENNA 15 July '99 (4+7)   (2+5)
Büro 1 @ Le GARAGE, Paris 10·5·98 (8)
EDITED AT BADY Studio, Vienna, dolby EAST 1, VIENNA
& steam Room CHicago July 1999
C in Circle 1999 MEGO

Artwork & photographic representation of Fenn o'berg
by chicks on speed   corrected by pita

add n to (x)
avant hard

cd front & images from
cd reverse
overleaf: 12" inner
spread
design: add n to (x)
band photography:
joe dilworth
mute
1999

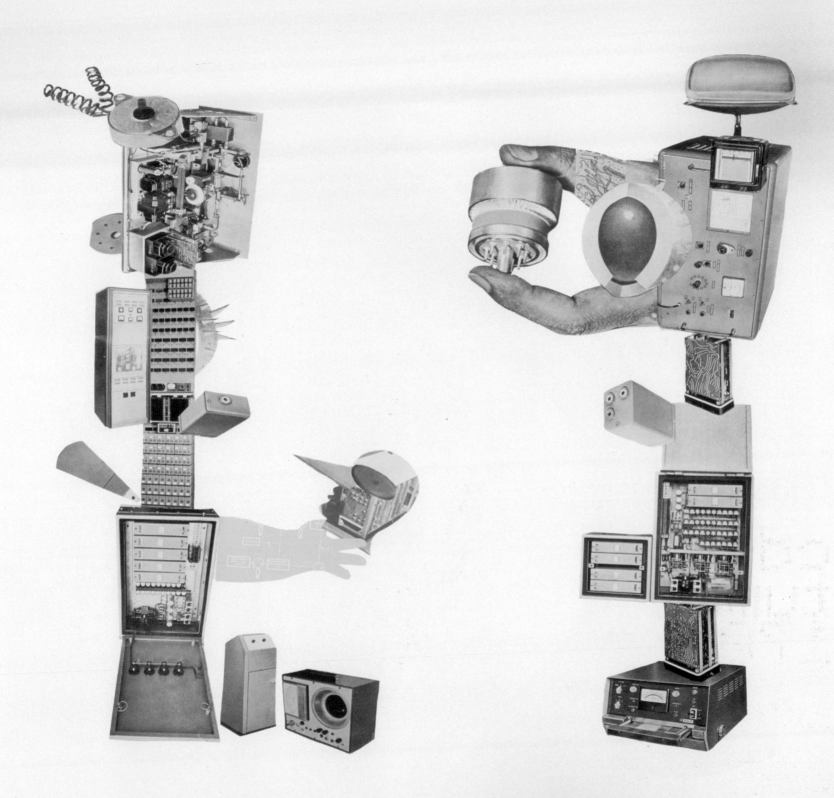

fennesz
plus forty seven
degrees 56' 37"
minus sixteen degrees
51' 08"

cd packaging (front &
fold open inner)
overleaf: cd booklet
spreads
design & photography:
jon wozencroft
touch
1999

5 027803 144026

fennesz

plus forty seven degrees 56' 37"
minus sixteen degrees 51' 08"

phoenecia
odd jobs

cd front. opposite: cd
inner spread & reverse
tray details
design: arnold · full
circle@angelfire.com
the schematic music
company
1999

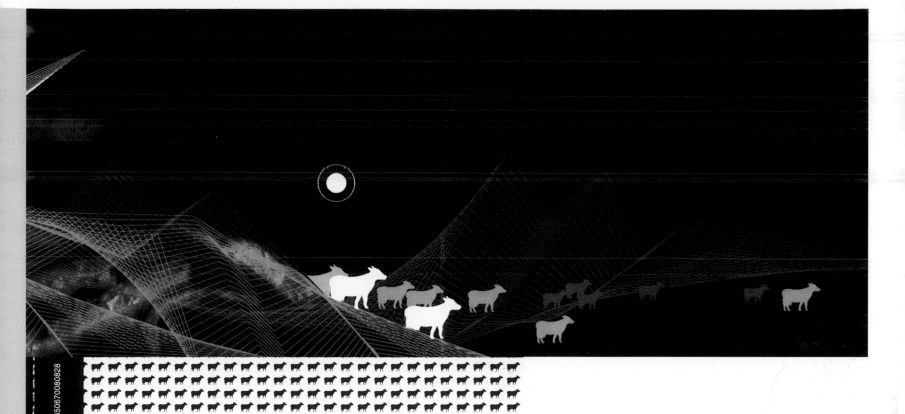

650670080828

PHOENECIA ODD.JOBS

PHOENECIA **ODD.**

1. **soul oddity**   get fresh
2. **soul oddity**   rhythm bo
3. autechre   systems
4. richard devine   skinpeel
5. ectomorph & godfather   version
6. push button objects   citrus car
7. takeshi muto   ketalonia

6 50670 08082 8

© 1999 the schematic music company™

>sch. 8X8

all songs published by light of man/bmi
Original version written and produced by J. Kay _ R. Delcastillo
all xx chrome ozone holders send pict files to us@schematic.net

design.Arnold • full circle@angelfire.com

phoenecia
randa roomet

cd front & reverse
design: the designers
republic
warp
1997

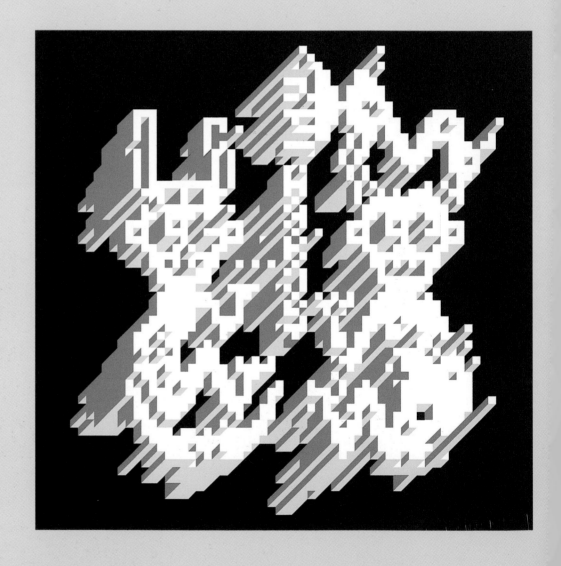

WAP98CD. LC2070. 1X44.1. PHOENECIA. RANDA ROOMET.
01SOMORY. 02Y-INTERCPNKT. 03THONG. 04CAN. KAY-DEL CASTILLO 50-50. LIGHT OF MAN. BMI.
℗ 1997 WARP RECORDS LTD. © 1997 WARP RECORDS LTD. PO BOX 474 SHEFFIELD S1 3BW. MADE IN ENGLAND.
http://www.warp-net.com http://www.thedesignersrepublic.com

ENTRYCODE 5021603098022.

FIRST RELEAS
ALSO AVAILAB

WAP98CD. LC2070. PHOENECIA. RANDA ROOMET.

ENTRYCODE 5021603098022.

PRMLSCRM
XTRMNTR

primal scream
exterminator

cd booklet spreads
design: house @ intro
creation
2000

creation
3235

primal scream
exterminator

cd booklet spreads
design: house @ intro
creation
2000

cornelius
fantasma

cd front
designer:
masakazu kitayama
art director:
mitsuo shindo
matador records
1998

performed by CORNELIUS produced by KEIGO OYAMADA
matador menu./OLE 300 compact disc digital audio stereo

ole3
1929

cornelius
chapter 8 – seashore
and horizon

cd front & inner detail
designer: masakazu
kitayama (help!) &
cornelius
matador records
1998

Attention :

How to enjoy "STAR FRUITS SURF RIDER"

01. Prepare two CD players and one mixer.
(Please purchase one if you don't have one)
02. Place "STAR FRUITS" on one CD player.
03. Place "SURF RIDER" on the other CD player.
04. Set the balance of the CD mixer to the middle.
05. Use the headphones to enjoy a higher quality of sound.
06. Pause the CD player on track 3. Slightly press the play button.
07. Take a deep breath and relax your mind.
(Think of fresh steaming Pancakes to get all other thoughts off your mind.)
08. Be casual, like cookies being offered with coffee,
and press the play button .
09. You are now listening to "STAR FRUITS SURF RIDER"
10. If the timing is off, slowly adjust the rotation speed by hand.
11. Now close your eyes and imagine yourself surfing in a night sky full of stars.
If it doesn't work at first, keep trying until it does.

"STAR FRUITS SURF RIDER" の楽しみ方

01. CDプレイヤーを2台とミキサーを1台用意して下さい。
(持っていない方はお買い求め下さい。)
02. "STAR FRUITS" をCDプレイヤーの1台にのせて下さい。
03. 次に "SURF RIDER" をもう1台のCDプレイヤーにのせて下さい。
04. CDプレイヤーのミキサーのバランスをまん中に合わせて下さい。
05. ヘッドフォンをお使いになると、より望ましい効果が得られます。
06. 両方のCDの曲をトラック3に設定しし、プレイボタンに手をそえて下さい。
07. 深呼吸をし、精神統一をします。(すべての雑念を取り払うため、
美味しく焼けたホットケーキを想像して下さい。)
08. コーヒーに添えられたクッキーのようなさりげなさをイメージしながら、
同時にプレイボタンを押します。
09. "STAR FRUITS SURF RIDER" が聞こえ始めます。
10. タイミングが合わない場合は少し手で調整してくれ。
11. 満天の星空をサーフィンするあなたの姿を想像しながら、目を閉じてみましょう。
最初に合わせられなくても、あきらめず何度もトライして下さい。

Cornelius / Star Fruits Surf Rider

...er (radio edit)
...er (remix by Damon Albarn)

...nelius

...tayama (HELP!) & Cornelius

SFSR

cornelius
star fruits surf rider

cd fronts & inner detail
designer: masakazu
kitayama & cornelius
matador records
1998

Cornelius / Star Fruits Surf Rider

O1 Star Fruits Surf Rider (single version)
O2 Ball In -Kick Off
O3 Star Fruits Green
All songs and lyrics written by Cornelius,

Sleeve designed by Masakazu Kitayama (HELP!) & Cornelius

SFSR

tahiti 80
puzzle

cd foldout details
design & illustration:
laurent fetis
atmospheriques
1999

Orbital   The Middle
                       Of Nowhere

orbital
the middle of nowhere

cd spreads
design: farrow design
photography: louise
kelly & orbital
ffrr
1999

fcd3
98

orbital
style

cd fronts
design: farrow design
photography: louise
kelly
ffrr
1999

estr brinkmann
totes rennen
maschine 8:02
on ne vit pas 5:33
zeichenkette 6:37
feranloop 9:10
se mouvoir 6:22
mimesis 4:46
brinkmann totes rennen

estr brinkmann totes rennen
16

supposé 07

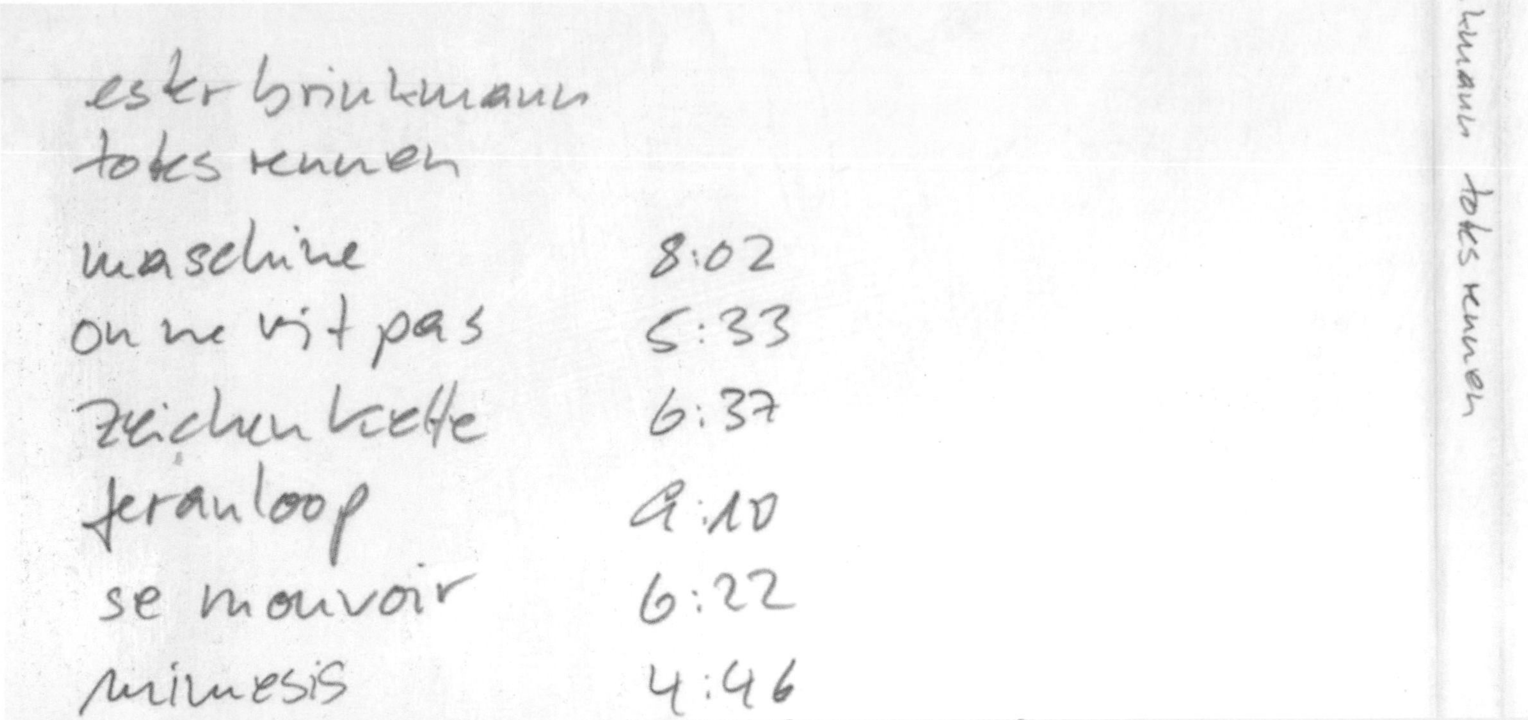

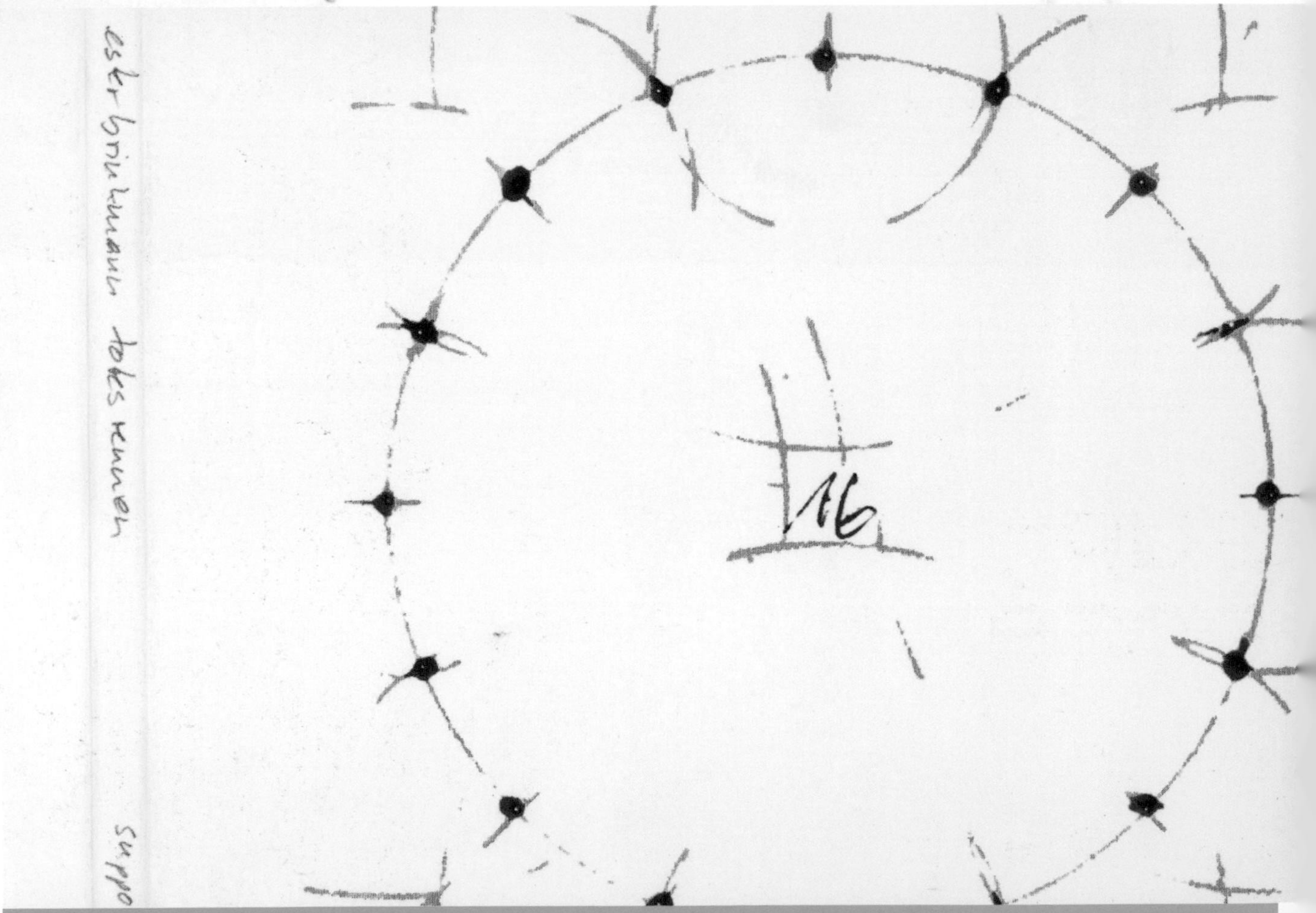

ester brinkmann
totes rennen

cd digipack front & reverse
idea: klaus sander
drawing: thomas brinkmann
font: ayat theismann
realization: uwe hecker
supposé
1998

sup-
posé

ester brinkmann
weisse nächte

cd digipack front & cd
label
idea: thomas brinkmann
& klaus sander
writing: ayat theismann
realization: uwe hecker
supposé
1999

pauline oliveros /
david gamper
at the ijsbreker

cd front & back
design: meeuw
jdk productions
1999

p.o. box 92097
1090 AB Amsterdam
The Netherlands
fax: ..31 20 66 30 559
e: jdkprod@xs4all.nl

5400711000408

pauline oliveros

david gamper

at the ijsbreker

jan 24, 1999

PALM DESERT

ecd 017

van dyke parks + itchy
pet, honey barbara,
elliott peter earls
palm desert

cover & inner spreads
design & photography:
rudy vanderlans
emigre music
1999

never-never la

Juxtaposed to B.B.D. and O.

xdus tcha

the chemical brothers
surrender

cd inner spread
design: mark tappin
@ blue source
illustration: kate gibb
virgin records
1999

the chemical brothers
music: response

cd front
design: mark tappin
@ blue source
illustration: kate gibb
virgin records
1999

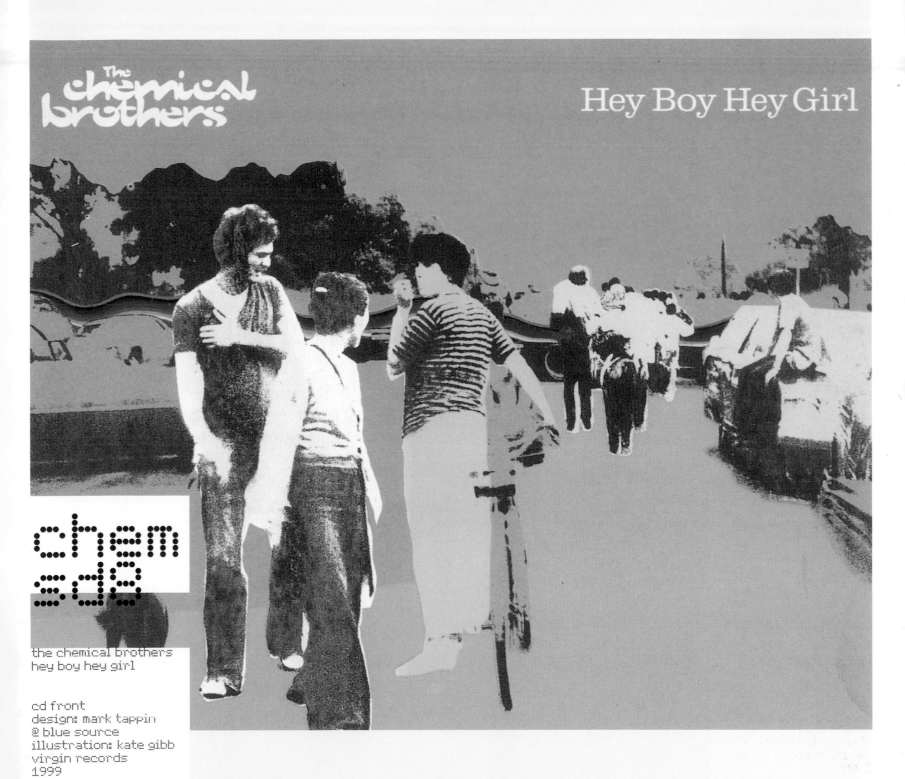

The Chemical Brothers

Hey Boy Hey Girl

chem
sgs

the chemical brothers
hey boy hey girl

cd front
design: mark tappin
@ blue source
illustration: kate gibb
virgin records
1999

**rcd2
002**

arne nordheim
electric

cd front/back & cd
booklet detail
design: kim hiorthøy
rune grammofon
1998

**solitaire
pace
warszawa
polypoly
colorazione**

originally released in 1974
℗ + © 1985 norsk komponistforening
℗ + © 1998 rune grammofon as

RCD 2002
all rights reserved

7 033662 020027

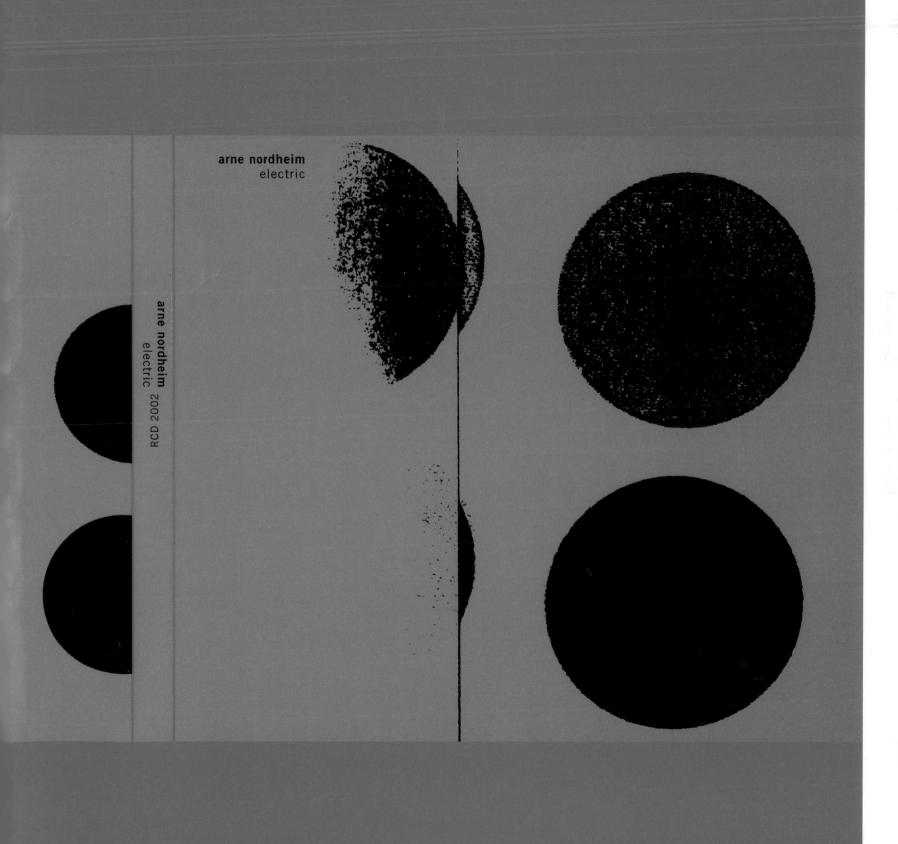

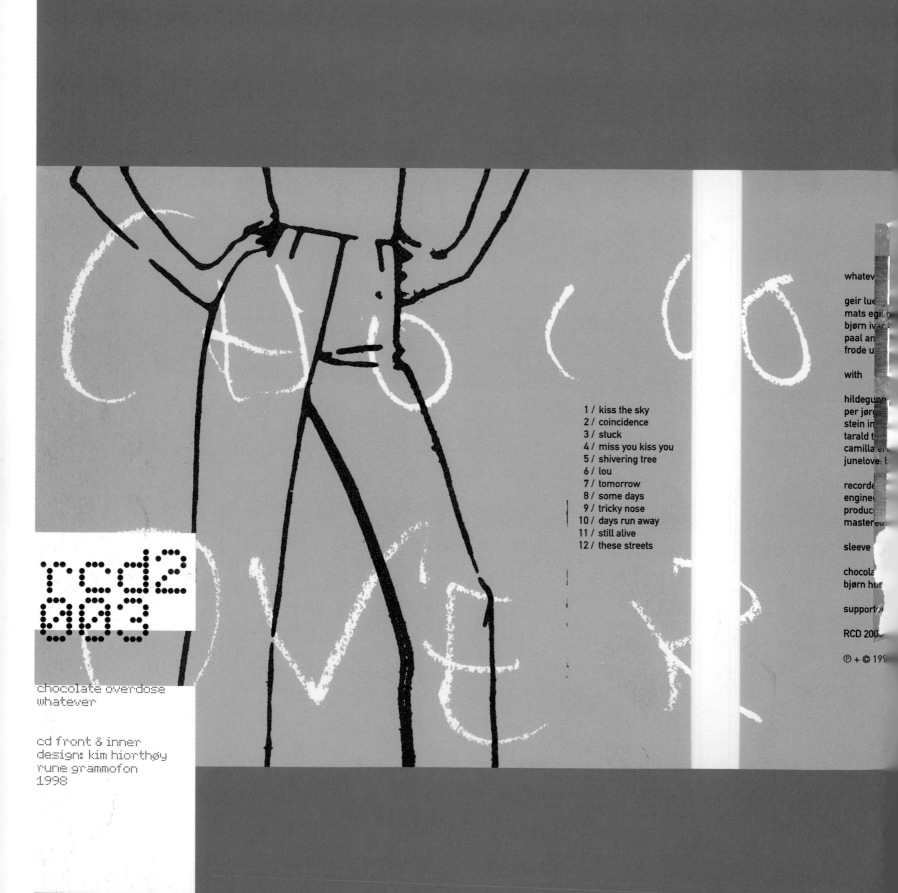

1 / kiss the sky
2 / coincidence
3 / stuck
4 / miss you kiss you
5 / shivering tree
6 / lou
7 / tomorrow
8 / some days
9 / tricky nose
10 / days run away
11 / still alive
12 / these streets

whatev

geir lue
mats egil g
bjørn ivar
paal an
frode u

with

hildegunn
per jørg
stein in
tarald t
camilla e
junelove:

recorde
engine
produc
mastered

sleeve

chocola
bjørn hur

support

RCD 200

℗ + © 199

rcd2
003

chocolate overdose
whatever

cd front & inner
design: kim hiorthøy
rune grammofon
1998

whatever.

s, acoustic guitar
ead guitar, backing vocals, drums on 9
s, backing vocals, guitar on 9
ards
s, bass on 9

g vocals on 1
on 4
ms on 6 and 10
7
ng vocals on 9
s on 12

ding
y and bjørn ivar tysse
by chocolate overdose
jon as

orthøy

ld like to thank rod johnstad, aksel fug
maria andersen, musikkmiljø, v.t. sys

settavgiftsfond

mmofon as / chocolate overdose

jazzkammer timex RCD2014

rcd2
b14

1999
...ider morning
...press
...or breakfast
...necklace

...less thermo
...made of paper
happy new year

jazzkammer
timex

cd front/back & inner
detail
design: kim hiorthøy
rune grammofon
1999

33662 020140

jazzkammer
timex

information
phonophani
düplo
a threatened logical unit
arne nordheim
monolight
deathprod
plirk
supersilent
alog
furuholmen/bjerkestrand
marhaug / rishaug
biosphere/deathprod

love comes shining over the mountains RCD2012

www.runegrammofon.com

7 033662 020126

love comes shining
over the mountains

cd front/back & inner
detail
design: kim hiorthøy
rune grammofon
1999

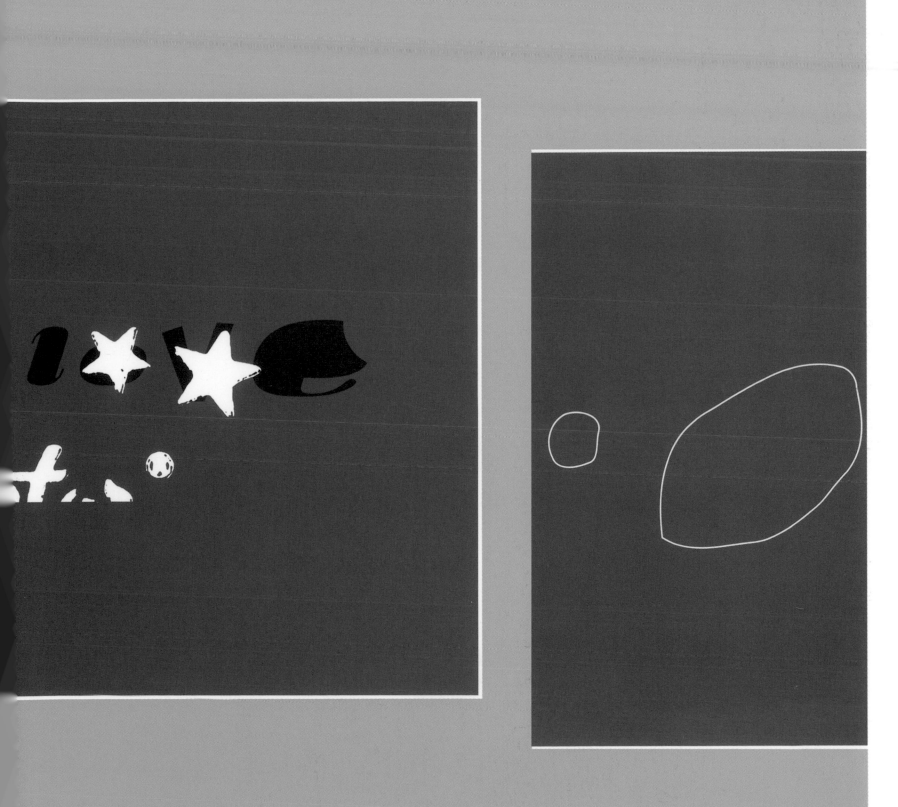

01 månelyst
02 reiseslått - til hans w. brimi (1918-1998)
03 straum
04 gråtaslag - etter siri dyvik/petter strømsing
05 skystudie
06 ikodne gjekk på vollen og slo - etter gunvor økland
07 svev - til eilif
08 biberslått - til heinrich ignaz franz biber (1644-1704)
09 understraum
10 var
11 rose
12 ondt
13 gorrlaus
14 akvarium
15 solformørkelse - steinsfjellet 11. august 99

nils økland straum

RCD2015

rcd2 6415

nils økland
straum

cd front/back & inner
detail
design: kim hiorthøy
rune grammofon
1999

3662 020157

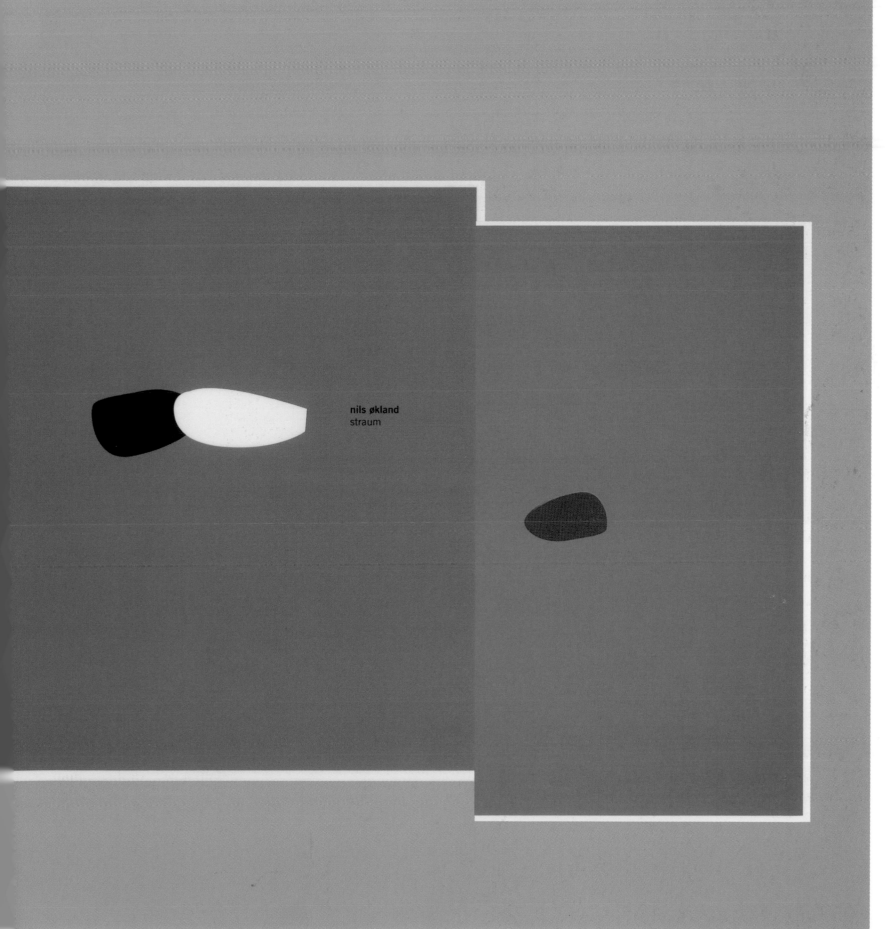

nils økland
straum

rcd2
009

www.runegrammofon.com

chocolate overdose
dingledoodies

cd front/back & inner
detail
design: kim hiorthøy
rune grammofon
1999

0096

chocolate overdose **dingledoodies**

RCD 2009

chocolate overdose **dingledoodies**

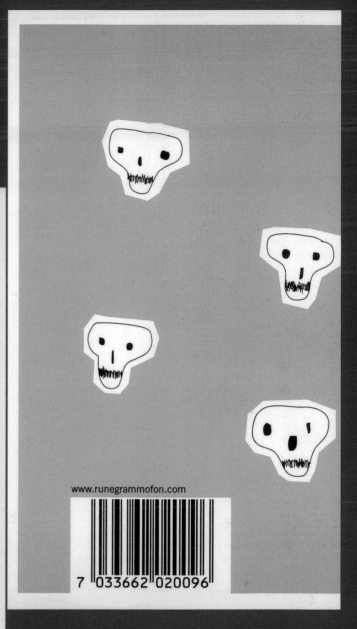

www.runegrammofon.com

7 033662 020096

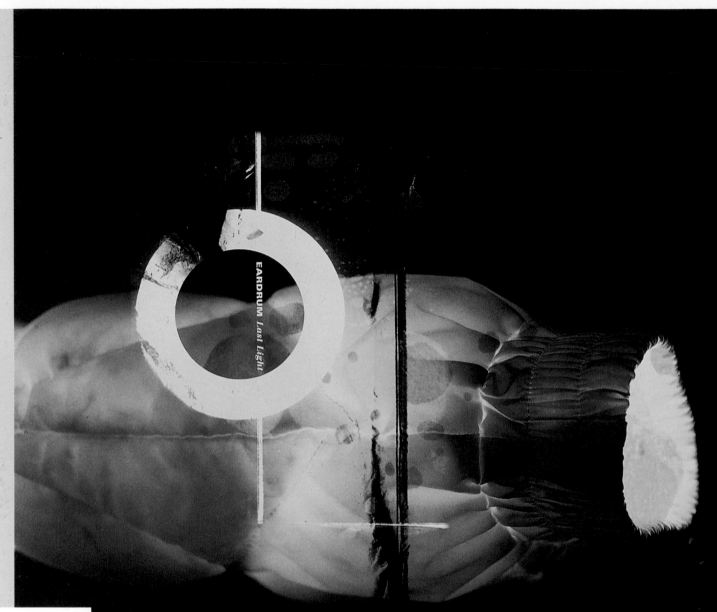

EARDRUM *Last Light*

bay
7v

eardrum
last light

12" front & reverse
detail
art & design: martin
andersen & chris bigg
art direction: v23
the leaf label
1999

EARDRUM *Last Light*

bays
cd

beige
i don't either

cd front & inner
spreads
art direction & design:
kjell ekhorn & jon forss
at ekhornforss
photography: simona
dell'agli & photodisc
the leaf label
2000

72 73

12one rec: demo3pack 4émoli
remixes: 5to rococo rot, 6dat politics7 fennesz8

tr
166

tone rec
demo pack démoli

cd front & inner spread
design: fred walheer
photography: tone rec
quatermass
2000

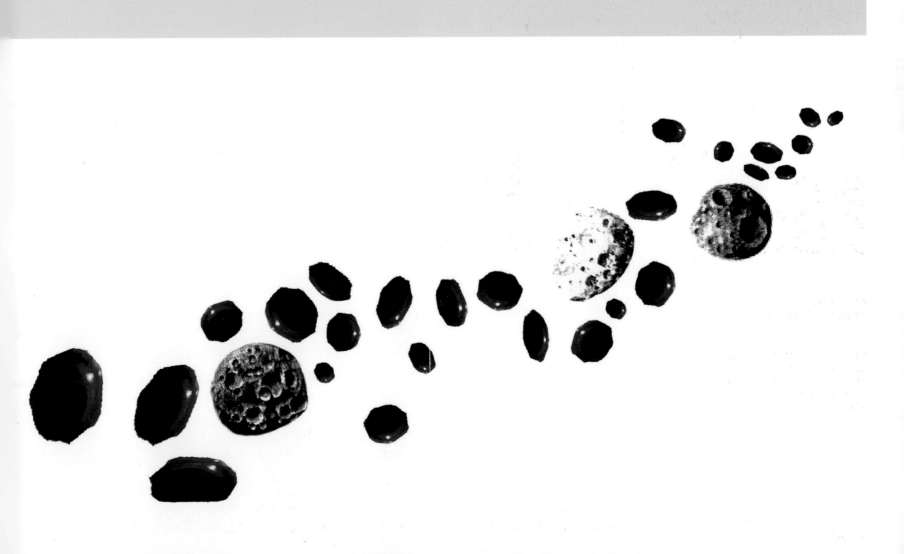

skull snapz

cd reverse, 12" front,
12" labels
design & art direction:
trevor jackson & jason
evans
photography: jason
evans
output recordings ltd
1999

SKULL
SNAPZ

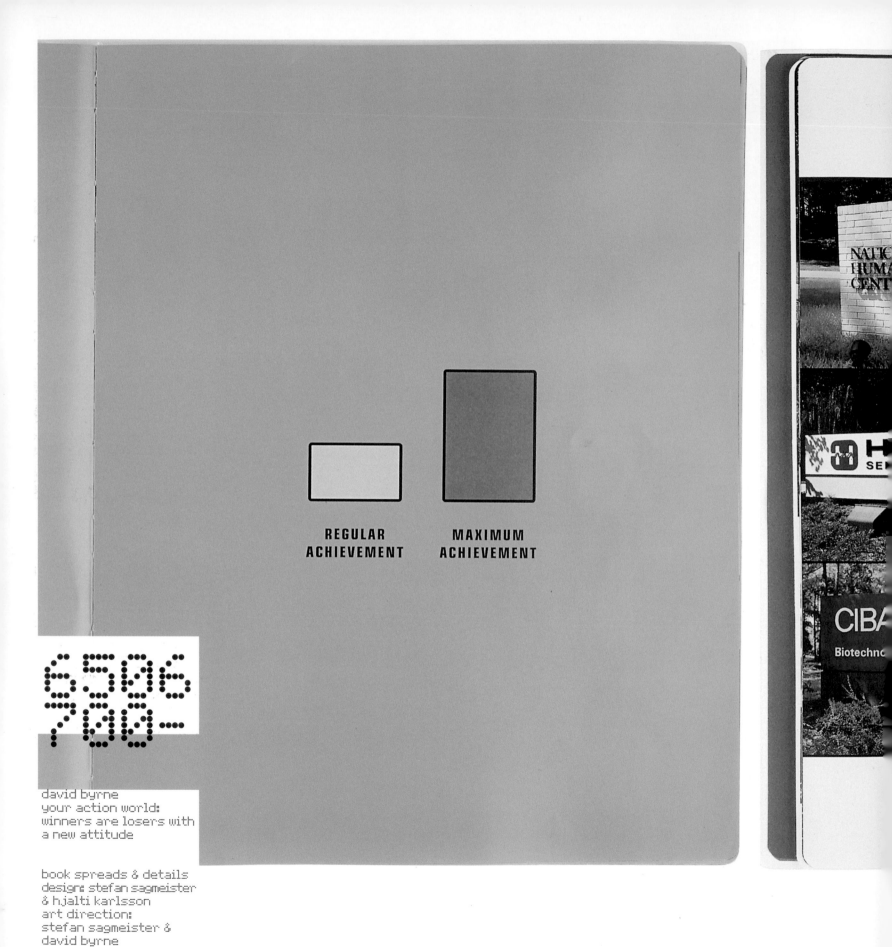

REGULAR
ACHIEVEMENT

MAXIMUM
ACHIEVEMENT

6506
700-

david byrne
your action world:
winners are losers with
a new attitude

book spreads & details
design: stefan sagmeister
& hjalti karlsson
art direction:
stefan sagmeister &
david byrne
photography: david
byrne
sagmeister inc.
1999

ACTIVE

PROACTIVE

6506
700-

david byrne
your action world:
winners are losers with
a new attitude

book spreads & details
design: stefan sagmeister
& hjalti karlsson
art direction:
stefan sagmeister &
david byrne
photography: david
byrne
sagmeister inc.
1999

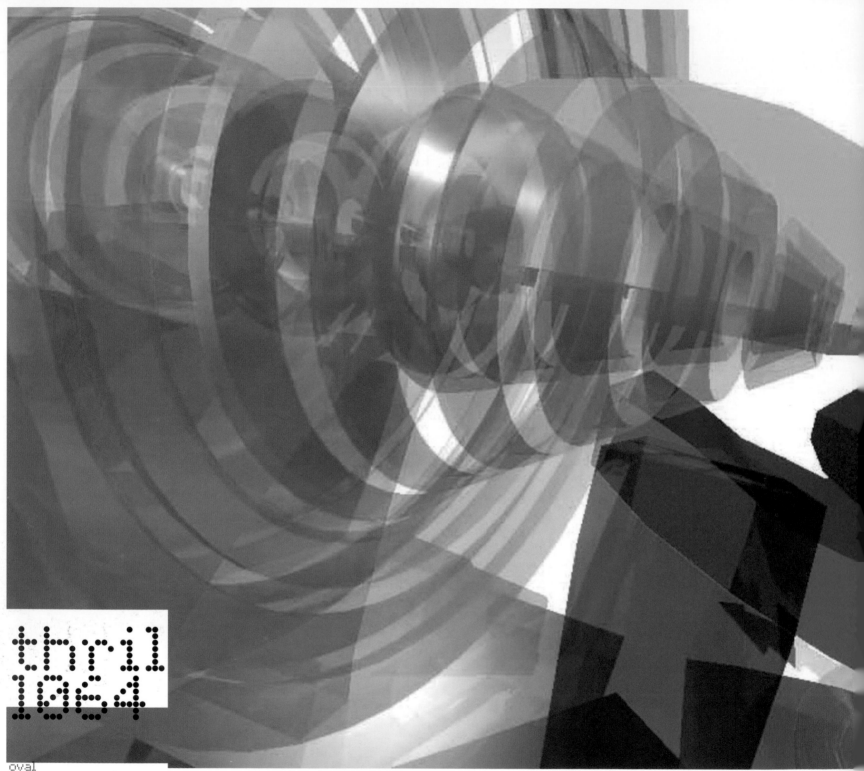

thrill
1924

oval
szenariodisk

cd front/back & inner
design: frieda luczak
at icon kommunikations-
design
thrill jockey
1999

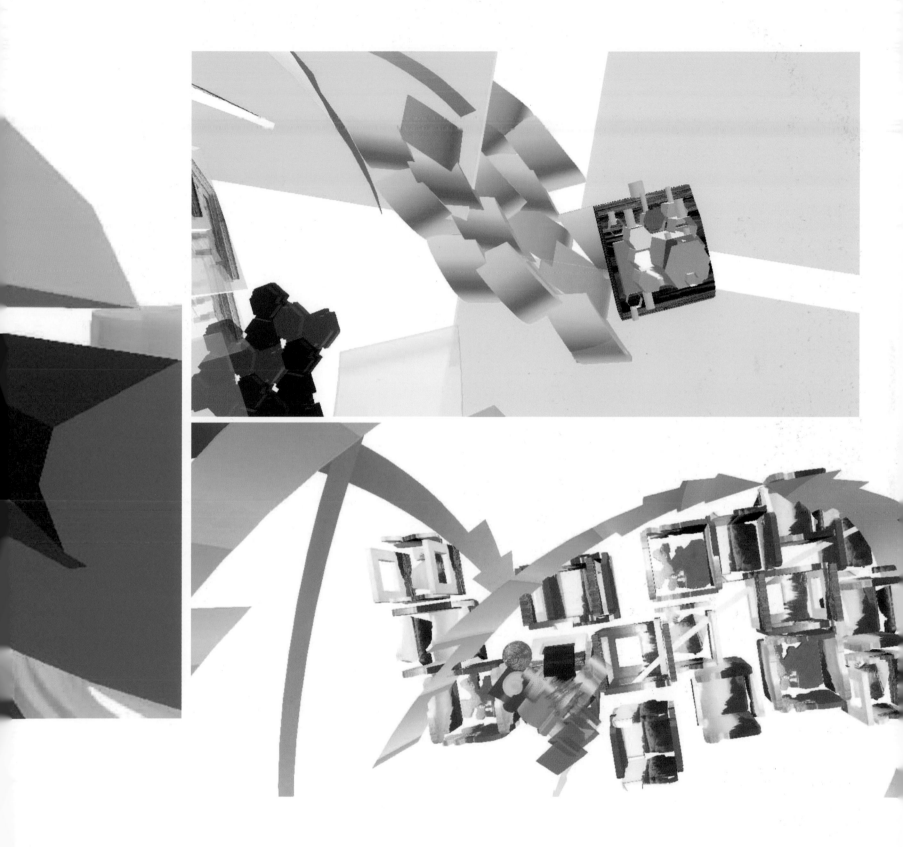

SPEC .
taylor deupree + richard chartier

12k: www.12k.com • taylor@12k.com • 12k1007 • **limited:500**

taylor deupree &
richard chartier
'spec.'

cd front & back
design: taylor deupree
12k
1999

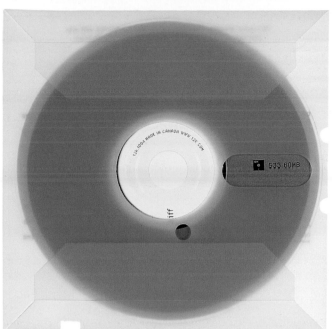

12k1
004

various
.aiff

cd front & back
design: taylor deupree
package design:
dan abrams
12k
1999

einstürzende neubauten

silence is sexy

einstürzende neubauten

silence is sexy

Pelikanol 18:30

cds- tumm

einstürzende neubauten
silence is sexy

cd front & inner
packaging
design: gerwin schmidt/
béla stetzer (with blixa
bargeld)
photography:
anno dittmer
mute
2000

86 87

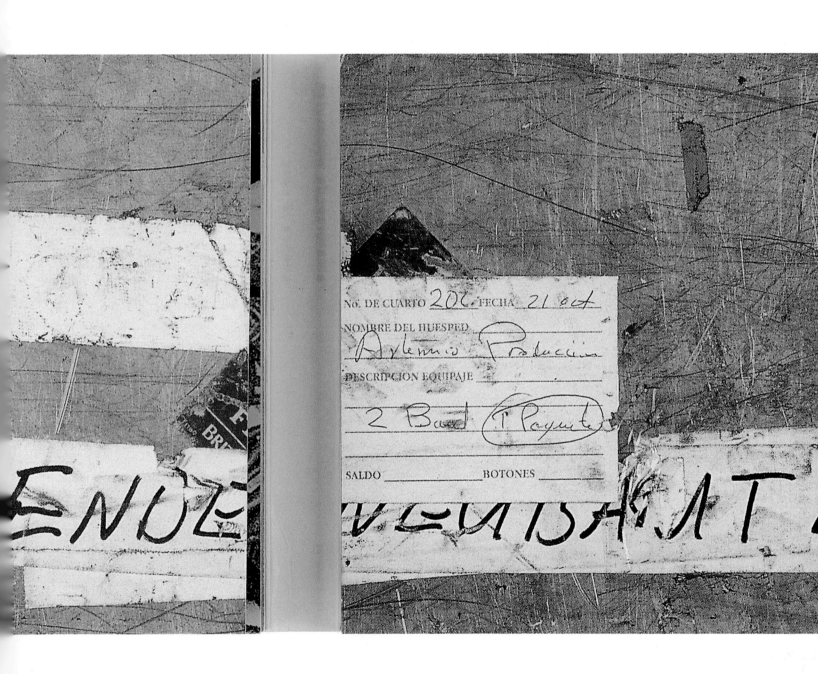

TO LOSE LA TREK

KICK OFF!

pias ycan le

campag velocet
bon chic bon genre

cd booklet spreads &
reverse tray
design: the designers
republic
photography:
david bailey 8 & dr tm
pias
1999

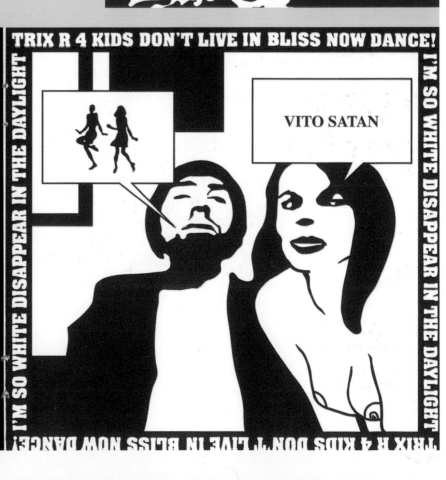

isotope ²¹⁷°
THE UNSTABLE MOLECULE

isotope 217
the unstable molecule

cd front
design: andy mueller at
ohio girl co.
cover painting by
eugene lloyd
thrill jockey
1997

thrill
1064

isotope 217°
utonian_automatic

cd inner detail
art direction & design:
andy mueller at ohiogirl
collage by eugene lloyd
thrill jockey
1999

isotope 217° : utonian

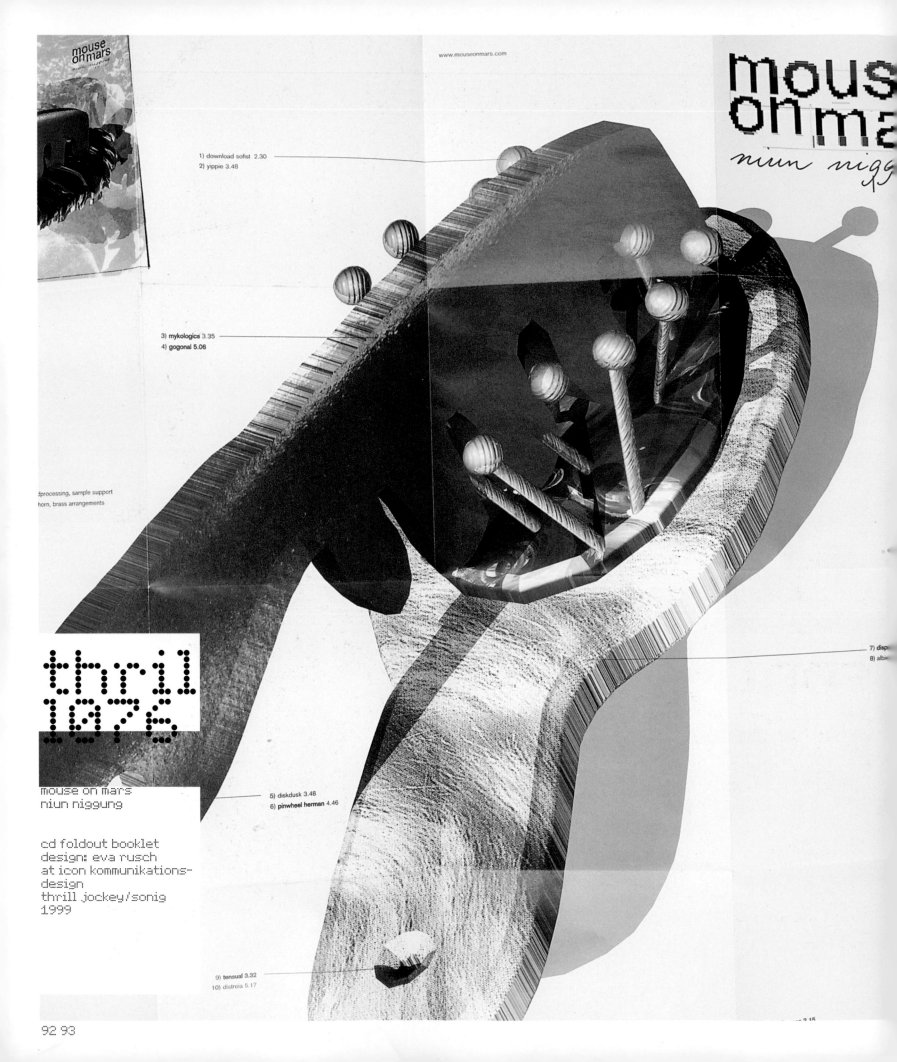

mouse on mars

www.mouseonmars.com

mous
on ma
niun nigg

1) download sofist 2.30
2) yippie 3.48

3) mykologics 3.35
4) gogonal 5.06

processing, sample support
horn, brass arrangements

thrill
1072

mouse on mars
niun niggung

cd foldout booklet
design: eva rusch
at icon kommunikations-
design
thrill jockey/sonig
1999

5) diskdusk 3.48
6) pinwheel herman 4.46

7) disp
8) albi

9) tensual 3.32
10) distroia 5.17

soni
aus
blau

various
sonig comp.

cd foldout booklet
design: frieda luczak
at icon kommunikations-
design
sonig, köln,
thrill jockey
2000

ew20
2

mellow
instant love

picture disc artwork
detail
design & illustration:
laurent fetis
atmospheriques
1999

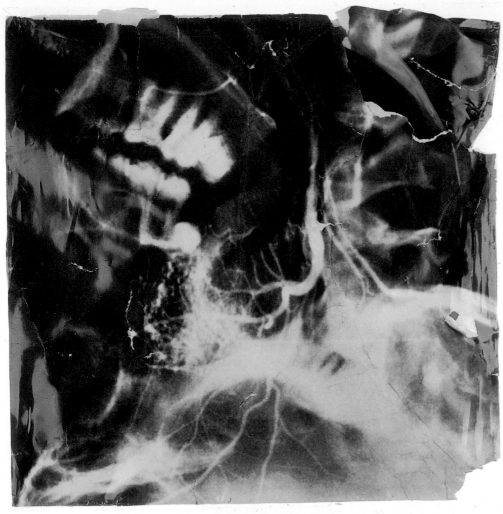

ICARUS U

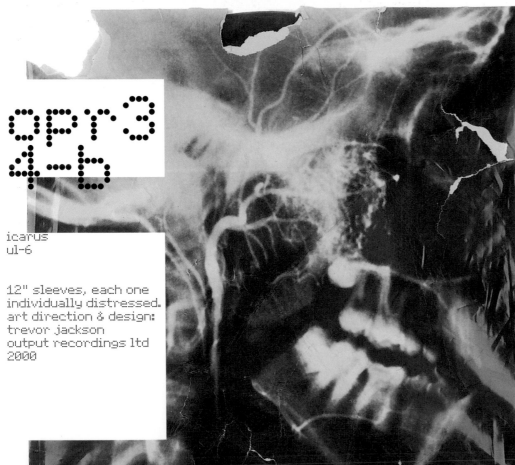

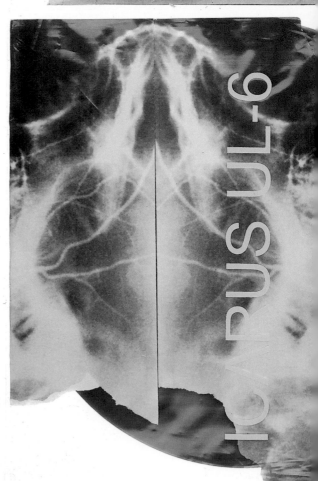
ICARUS UL-6

output
426

icarus
ul-6

12" sleeves, each one
individually distressed.
art direction & design:
trevor jackson
output recordings ltd
2000

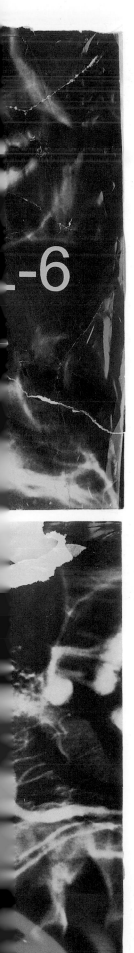
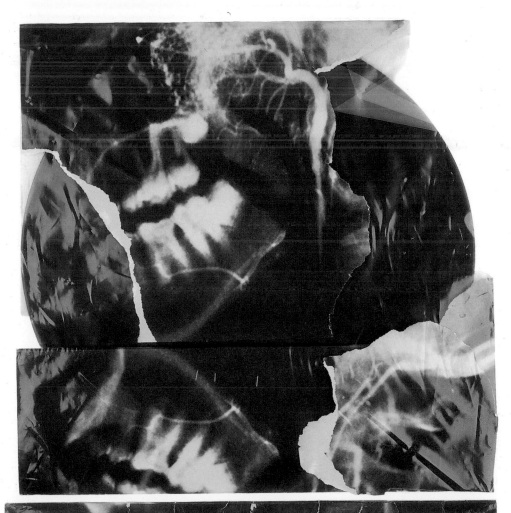
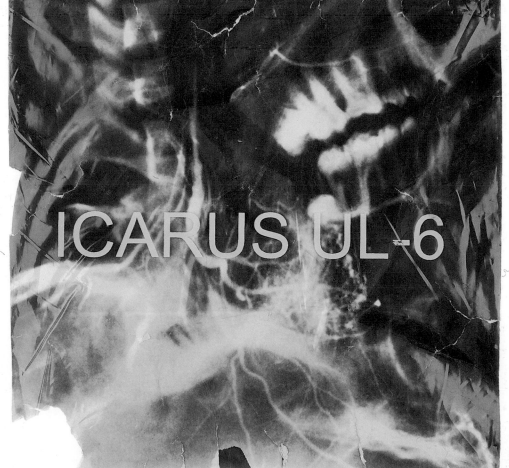

ICARUS UL-6

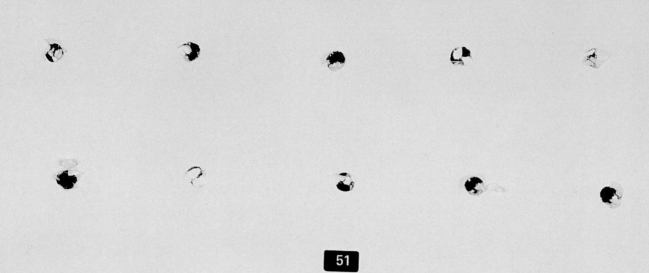

51

christoph de babalon/
kid 606
split series #10

12" outer sleeve with
hand drilled holes
design: obsessive eye
holes: cawley/cruisey/
howell/knight
fat cat recordings
2000

298

team doyobi/
req
split series #14

12" outer sleeve with
hand drilled holes
design: obsessive eye
holes: cawley/cruisey/
howell/knight
fat cat recordings 2000

gramme

12" front & back with
sticker
art direction & design:
trevor jackson
photography:
donald christie
output recordings ltd
1999

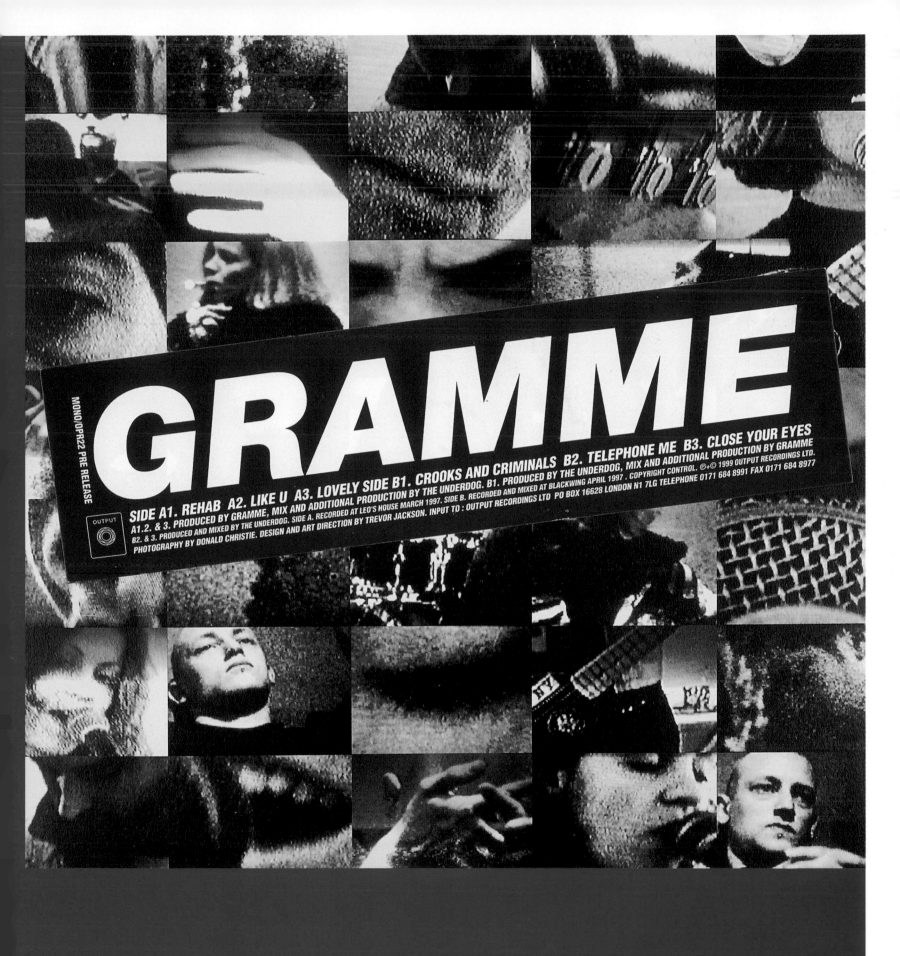

GRAMME

MONO/OPR22 PRE RELEASE

OUTPUT

SIDE A1. REHAB A2. LIKE U A3. LOVELY SIDE B1. CROOKS AND CRIMINALS B2. TELEPHONE ME B3. CLOSE YOUR EYES
A1.2. & 3. PRODUCED BY GRAMME, MIX AND ADDITIONAL PRODUCTION BY THE UNDERDOG. B1. PRODUCED BY THE UNDERDOG, MIX AND ADDITIONAL PRODUCTION BY GRAMME
B2. & 3. PRODUCED AND MIXED BY THE UNDERDOG. SIDE A. RECORDED AT LEO'S HOUSE MARCH 1997. SIDE B. RECORDED AND MIXED AT BLACKWING APRIL 1997 . COPYRIGHT CONTROL. ℗+© 1999 OUTPUT RECORDINGS LTD.
PHOTOGRAPHY BY DONALD CHRISTIE. DESIGN AND ART DIRECTION BY TREVOR JACKSON. INPUT TO : OUTPUT RECORDINGS LTD PO BOX 16628 LONDON N1 7LG TELEPHONE 0171 684 8991 FAX 0171 684 8977

110.9   **LUKE SLATER**   **WIRELESS**

NOMU70CD

novamute

Written, produced, recorded, mixed and arranged by
Luke Slater at Space Station e, UK. Mastered by Nils/
Graeme at the Exchange. Vocals by Speech Recognition.
Guitar by Seth Hodder. Additional drums by Luke Slater
and Alan Sage. 'In the Pocket' contains a sample of
'Rocket in the Pocket' (Cerrone) © Island Music Ltd
'Sum Tom Tin' contains a sample of 'Funky Mule' (Holmes/
Harris/Turner/Holmes) © Wilhos Music Publishing.
Art direction and design by House at Intro. Photography
by Nigel Bennett.
Published by Mute Song. ℗ & © 1999 Mute Records
Ltd. Mail order available from Mute Bank 429 Harrow
Road, London W10 4RE. Send s.a.e. or phone 24 hour
credit card hotline ++44 (0) 20 8964 0029 or fax
++44 (0) 20 8964 3722. Mute - http://www.mute.co.uk.
Distributed by Vital. Made in Great Britain.

LSCD

110.9

**LUKE
SLATER**

WIRELESS

'...Polish vodka'. The gun disappeared and there
was a click. I strained my ears to listen to the
conversation as the tape reeled on insanely –
radio tuned to a dead station. Outside, the Sunbeam
started up – another click, a sharp hiss, bone
on concrete, two seconds to act. '...a lot of dead
ends. And what about the operation?'

luke slater
wireless

cd digipack front,
reverse & inner detail

art direction & design:
house @ intro
photography: nigel
bennett
mute records ltd
1999

OR
SOME
COMPUTER
MUSIC

Aphex Twin
Beautyon
cd_slopper
General Magic
Kevin Drumm
Stephen Travis Pope
Trevor Wishart
Ubik
Zbigniew Karkowski
& Kasper T. Toeplitz

or made in england ISSUE 1

5 027803 330726

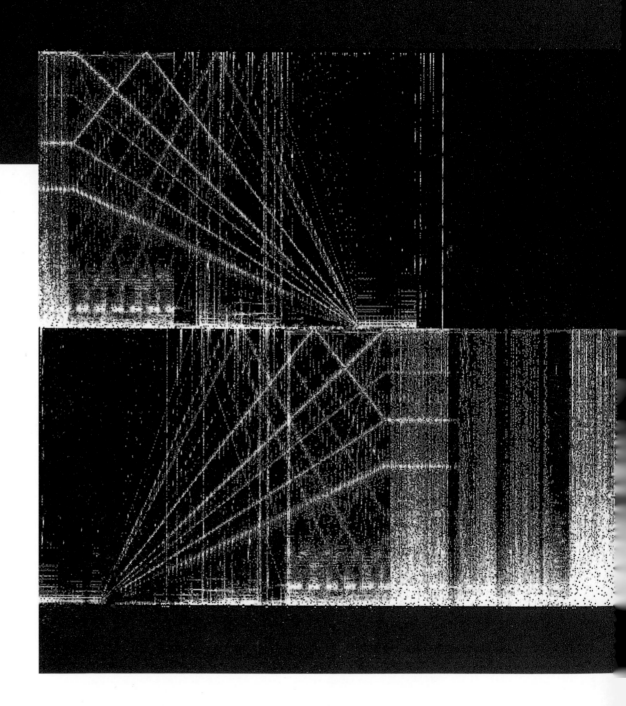

various
or some computer music

cd front, reverse tray
& inner spreads
design: russell haswell
or
1999

```
cd_slopper: "BLR     OODGR, ˆ 1:3"

header distracted by hack/ost 03.1999 using various software:

"sonderzeichen aussortiert,  eiger/ortler/unicode"

---------------------------------------------------------------------


    _€__+___#_)_                      :_$85_,_"_=1;_
2c_@__<_€___`_                         1;2c1;2c1;2c1;2c1;2c1;2c
    _@_)__;'_m_).? ?_%.
___X_&_X_|_X_<_                                          _
          _:_=_|_L|_:_?_*X_{_\_%_<_                        _
_^_=___%_____?_$_%_X_%___'_X_X_)+_&_\|_`
'_X_)_                              _?_+`_'
_)__|_+_`___+)_<_{f_"_#_|_|_X___%___?>_<___:_<_'_@_<__X
@__x_'_'_%___/___'_(_'___':_)_"_|_+_;__%_€_X_$_<__
_x_"_._#_"_                          _:_$_")_+_+_|_X_'_
_)_X__._'_   _<_%_S_'__<_%_x_|_X_'_
          _@_<__'___|_[_x_'_)_                  _<_x_'_x_
__"_x_'_)_>__?__+__?_=_#_]___+_X_$_`_f_
_^_'_%_+_1)_=_'_X_X_€_"_,_+_[___€_%_"____'<_+_?_'___
                              _+__)__+_)_<_+_$_+_\
_\_[_€_X_*_+_`_<_x_'___'_'_|_€_x_____.__
_x`    _X___L?_=_'__<_€_<_%_`_'X_S_+_x_
   _    _|_^__(__)_              &nbs>


Transfer interrupted!


;_                          _
_<_#_)_%__^_S____$_@__=__x_'
&_S_&_X_S_(_&__)__<_X_L:_'_&__$_'_/___+_)_|_`_)_<_"_$_
(_
```

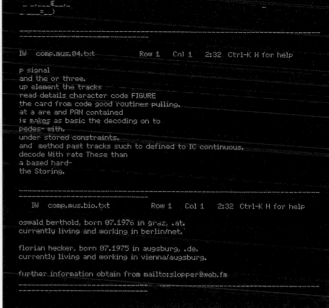

```
_  __/__€__/_
_ _/_/___€___/_
___=_}_)

-----------------------------------------------------------
------------------------------------------------------------

IW   comp.mus.04.txt            Row 1    Col 1    2:32  Ctrl-K H for help

P signal
and the or three.
up element the tracks
read details character code FIGURE
the card from code good routines pulling.
at a are and PAN contained
is makes as basic the decoding on to
pedes- with.
under stored constraints.
and  method past tracks such to defined to IC continuous.
decode With rate These than
a based hard-
the Storing.


-----------------------------------------------------------

   IW   comp.mus.bio.txt         Row 1    Col 1    2:32  Ctrl-K H for help

oswald berthold, born 07.1976 in graz, .at.
currently living and working in berlin/net.

florian hecker, born 07.1975 in augsburg, .de.
currently living and working in vienna/augsburg.

further information obtain from mailto:slopper@web.fm
-----------------------------------------------------------
```

Und die Fra- gen sind die Sät- ze   Und die Fra-gen sind die Sät-ze

Prosodic Tree examples for the *length* and *sharpness* of a phrase

The lowest level of the score is six sound mixing scripts using a list of about 2000 "particle" sounds. The particles are either syllables or single-phoneme segments of the voices of the speakers at specified values of length and sharpness (magnitudes similar to duration and pitch, described below).

The score was managed using the MODE (Musical Object Development Environment) [4], a set of object-oriented support classes and tools for sound and music processing in the Smalltalk language. Several different graphical and textual formats were used for generating, managing and realising the score. These include: graphical melody/utterance editors; editors for spatial location trajectories; programmed event generator scripts; and tools for the derivation, editing and application of T-R trees.

The figures below show T-R tree editors; the upper part of the left-hand figure shows the prosodic stress tree for the given word, and the lower part shows its particles. (The German word *Dunkelkammergespräche* means "dark-room discussions" and is one of the central words and T-R trees of the piece.) One can edit and apply prosodic stress trees derived from the properties of recorded spoken utterances by editing the tree in the upper part of the view. The result can be written out to a file in the form of a script for the signal processing programs used for speech processing with MODE. The right-hand figure shows a more advanced editor, which supports browsing the many versions of trees for the same utterance, and organising them into larger gestures that form the composition.

Autechre
Peel Session

TX
13/10/95

autechre peel session

cd fronts
design: the designers
republic
warp
1999

The Black Dog TX
Peel Session 13/01/95

Boards Of Canada TX
Peel Session 21/07/98

Plaid TX
Peel Session 08/01/98

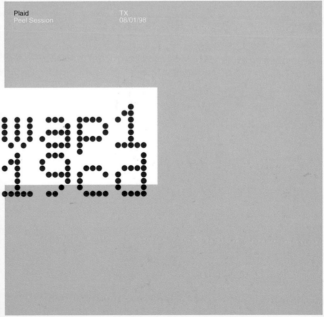

the black dog
peel session
boards of canada
peel session
plaid
peel session

cd fronts
design: the designers
republic
warp
1999

ast1
1cd

33.3

cd front & back
cover design:
jordana robinson
layout: mark owens
aesthetics
1998

BLOODCOUNT (DISCRETION)

None of the above

Would you rather I did it

do you have any references

tim berne
blood count discretion

cd front & inner detail
design: stephan byram
screwgun records
1999

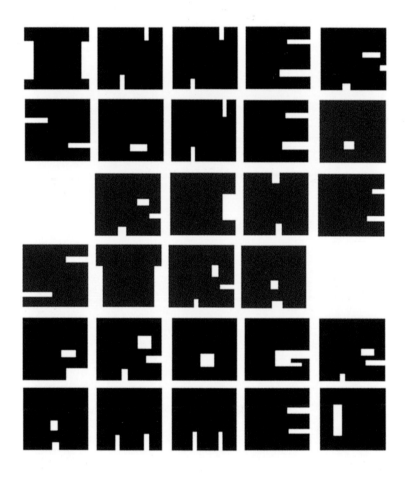

innerzone orchestra
programmed

cd front
design: subtle rukus
talkin' loud
1999

day one
waiting for a break
i'm doin' fine

stencil die cut
double 7" sleeves
design: tom hingston
melankolic/virgin
1999

Anton Bruhin   InOut

b3ta
=δ45

anton bruhin
inout

cd front
alga marghen
1999

1–3 Lucinda's Pastime (1962)   duration: **13'28"**
   Tape: kitchen sink at Sullivan Street apartment; Wollensak tape recorder

   1.   (duration: 06'04")
   2. "Andante Cantabile"   (duration: 05'05")
   3.   (duration: 02'19")

4   Memories: Performances (1963)   duration: **20'12"**
   Source material: various recordings; mixed at Bedford Street apartment

5   From Thaïs (1962)   duration: **09'42"**
   Recording: records into Wollensak tape recorders, mixed with Y-branch connector

6–9 Oracle, an electronic cantata on images of war: duration: **20'04"**
**   strike week version** (1962)
   Realization on various tape machines, in part with the help of James Tenney

   6. War Is Hell   (duration: 03'16")
   7. Sound-Off and March   (duration: 06'56")
   8. Black Hole   (duration: 04'01")
   9. Cried Silence   (duration: 05'51")

10 Flares – the electronic element (1963)   duration: **06'02"**
   Sounds generated at Columbia University Electronic Music Studio

11 Bev's Circus Tape (extract) (1962)   duration: **07'15"**
   Tape realization at Henry Street Playhouse: Alvin Nikolais'studio; assisted by James Seawright

philip corner
from the judson years

cd front & inner detail
photography:
george maciunas
alga marghen
1999

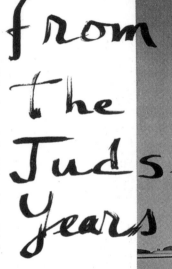

from the Judson Years

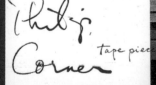
Philip Corner   tape pieces from the early 60s

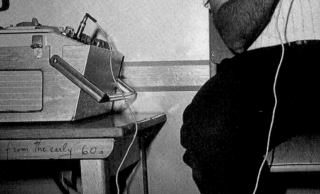

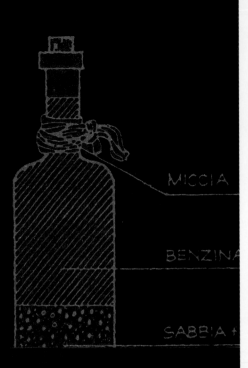

SLOW RIOT FOR NEW ZERØ KANADA E.P.

תֹ֫הוּ וָבֹ֫הוּ

4. 27 JEREMIAH

23 I beheld the earth,
   And, lo, it was waste and void;
   And the heavens, and they had
      no light.
24 I beheld the mountains, and, lo,
      they trembled,
   And all the hills moved to and
      fro.
25 I beheld, and, lo, there was no
      man,
   And all the birds of the heavens
      were fled.
26 I beheld, and, lo, the fruitful field
      was a wilderness,
   And all the cities thereof were
      broken down
   At the presence of the LORD,
   And before His fierce anger.
27 For thus saith the LORD:
   The whole land shall be desolate;
   Yet will I not make a full end.

23 רָאִ֙יתִי֙ אֶת־הָאָ֔רֶץ
וְהִנֵּה־תֹ֖הוּ וָבֹ֑הוּ
וְאֶל־הַשָּׁמַ֖יִם וְאֵ֥ין אוֹרָֽם׃
24 רָאִ֙יתִי֙ הֶֽהָרִ֔ים וְהִנֵּ֖ה רֹעֲשִׁ֑ים
וְכָל־הַגְּבָע֖וֹת הִתְקַלְקָֽלוּ׃
25 רָאִ֕יתִי וְהִנֵּ֖ה אֵ֣ין הָאָדָ֑ם
וְכָל־ע֥וֹף הַשָּׁמַ֖יִם נָדָֽדוּ׃
26 רָאִ֙יתִי֙ וְהִנֵּ֤ה הַכַּרְמֶל֙ הַמִּדְבָּ֔ר
וְכָל־עָרָ֗יו
נִתְּצוּ֙ מִפְּנֵ֣י יְהוָ֔ה
מִפְּנֵ֖י חֲר֥וֹן אַפּֽוֹ׃
27 כִּי־כֹה֙ אָמַ֣ר יְהוָ֔ה
שְׁמָמָ֥ה תִהְיֶ֖ה כָּל־הָאָ֑רֶץ
וְכָלָ֖ה לֹ֥א אֶעֱשֶֽׂה׃

godspeed you black
emperor
slow riot for new zerø
kanada e.p.

cd front & inner
design: godspeed you
black emperor
kranky
1999

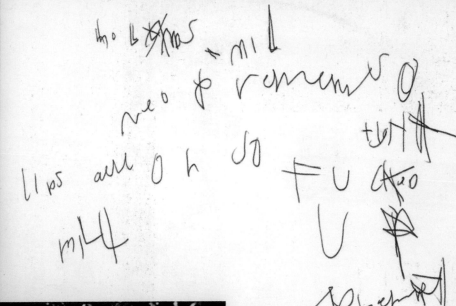

holland
neoprene so tight

cd front
design: uncredited
darla
1999

"Although the proposition that in the world we live in, effective action will necessarily be ruthless, ness; the question is whether one can sacrifice, for the sake of a hypothetical future, precisely th

joan of arc
live in chicago 1999

cd front & inner
spreads
art direction: joan of
arc, andy mueller &
j. gnewikow
design: j. gnewikow @
public
photography:
andy mueller / ohio girl
jade tree
1999

BROADCAST

THE NOISE MADE
BY PEOPLE

WARPCD65

warp
broadcast
the noise made by
people

cd front & booklet
spreads
design & photography:
house@intro
warp
2000

||||| ||||| ||||| S SONG FORBODING
PHRASES NOTES LIE LONG FRAME
THE SKY UNC|||||| |||| ||| |||||||
||||| |||||| T T |||||| ||| ||||||||
||||||||| |||||||||| THE SKY
UNCHANGING WINDOW|||| ||| || ||||||||
|||||||||||||| ERN TIED
WITH EVERY MEASURE SORROW FLIES

FRS WOVEN PATTERN TIED WITH
EVERY MEASURE SORROW||| ||||| |||||
||||||||||||||||||||||||||||||||||||

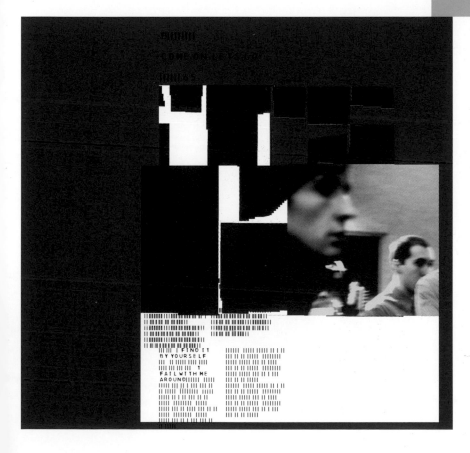

|||| I FIND IT
BY YOURSELF
||| || |||||| |||| T
FAIL WITH ME
AROUND||||| |||| || |||||

BARS THE |||||||||
THE
WIND WILL COME
BLOW| ANSWER
ECHOES ANSWER

||||| ||| |||||||
|||| RUN THE
MOUNTAIN
SCARRED BY
INVISIBLE

laurent garnier
unreasonable behaviour

cd front, inner tray &
booklet detail
design & illustration:
seb jarnot
pias
2000

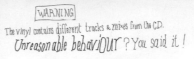

1 The Warning 1'48"
2 City sphere 6'15"
3 Forgotten thoughts 6'48"
4 The sound of the big babou 7'23"
5 Unreasonable behaviour 1'20"
6 Cycles d'oppositions 5'00"
7 The man with the red face 9'15"
8 Communications from the lab 5'14"
9 Greed (part 1+2) 6'48"
10 Dangerous drive 9'05"
11 Downfall 5'33"
12 Last tribute from the 20th century

F 115 CD
137 0115 20 / 381PS
CMV 5 0115 20 137 ACY
LC 07800 F

℗ 2000 F Communications
© 2000 F Communications
Released under license by PIAS Benelux, PIAS UK, PIAS Germany,
PLAYGROUND(Scandinavia), SO DENS (Spain), MUSIKVERTRIEB (Switzerland)
& FAMILY AFFAIR (Italy). Distribution in France by PIAS France, UK by Charged/VITA
& Germany by Connected. Export fax + 332 558 58 86. Made in Austria.
E-mail : fcom@wanadoo.fr F Communications : 20-22 rue Richer 75009 PAR

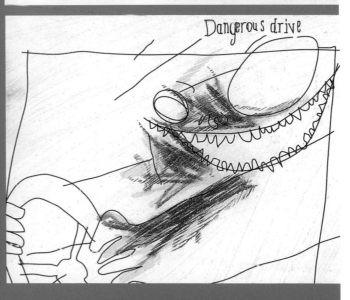

mwr1
9924

divine styler
wordpower2: directrix

cd front & inner wallet
concept & design:
ben drury
thermal photography:
sølve sundsbø
mowax
1999

DIVINE
STYLER

rza
as bobby digital

cd front & reverse
details
design: david calderley
art direction: rza &
david calderley
illustration: bill
sienkiewicz
v2/gee street
1999

m
je dis aime

cd front & inner tray
art direction, design
& photography: laurent
seroussi
m logo design: cyril
houplain
delabel
1999

gramm
personal_rock

cd front & foldout
section
design & photography:
jonas grossmann (env)
source records
1999

locd
ha37

gay dad
oh jim

cd front
graphic art by peter
saville, howard
wakefield & paul
hetherington. designed
at commercial art
london records 90 ltd
1999

gay dad
joy

cd front
graphic art by peter
saville, howard
wakefield & paul
hetherington. designed
at commercial art
london records 90 ltd
1999

gay dad
leisure noise

cd inner page
graphic art by peter
saville, howard
wakefield & paul
hetherington. designed
at commercial art
london records 90 ltd
1999

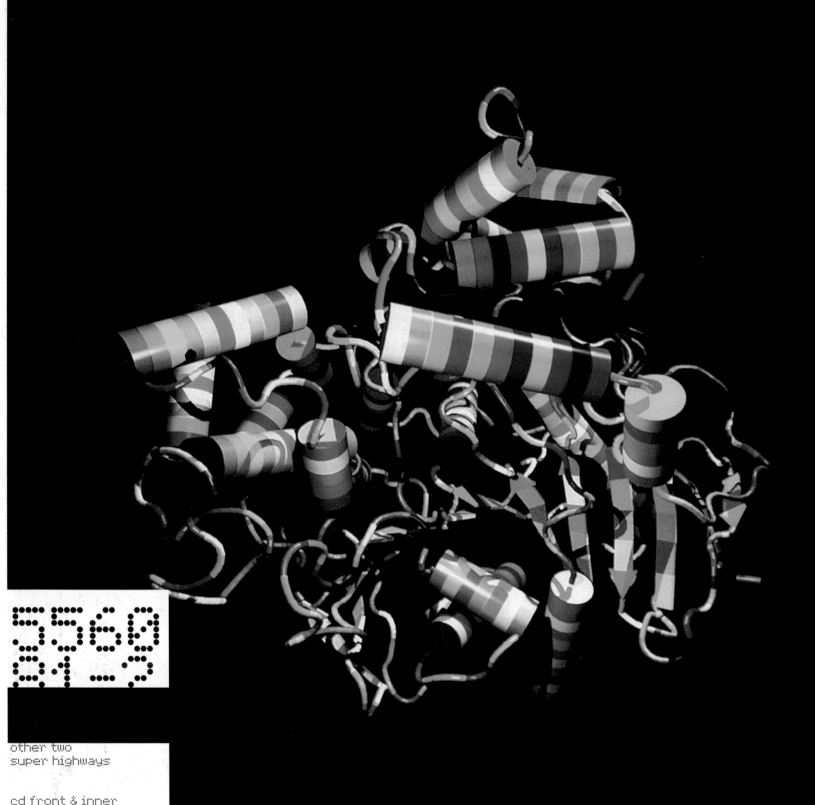

5569
8479

other two
super highways

cd front & inner
spreads
art direction: peter
saville
design: paul
hetherington & howard
wakefield at
commercial art
london records 90 ltd
1999

ecd0
12

itchy pet
dreaming out louder

cd box front. Box
containing cd/cd book &
feathers. Printed
wrap-around band.
design: rudy
vanderlans
box design: gail
swanlund
emigre music
1999

DREAMING OUT LOUDER

warp
p72a

autechre
ep7

transparent cd jewel
case with embossed
logo. cd detail
design: the designers
republic
warp
1999

RYOJI IKEDA
MORT AUX VACHES
1 HEADPHONICS [VPRO VERSION] :: +/- [VPRO VERSION]
2 LSDS
RODUCED   ND PERFORMED BY RYOJI IKEDA. RECORDED
APRIL 15,   998. COMMISSIONED BY VPRO RADIO   RE
AVONDEN'. THANKS > BERRIE KAMER AND JAN H OONX
STAALPI AT, P.O.BOX 11453, 1001 GL AMSTERD M.THE
NETH LANDS, P.O.BOX 83296, PORTLAND, OR 97 3,USA
   CeVE BY ALORENZ, BERLIN.THIS IS A LIMITED DITION
YOUR NUMBER: 098 /1000

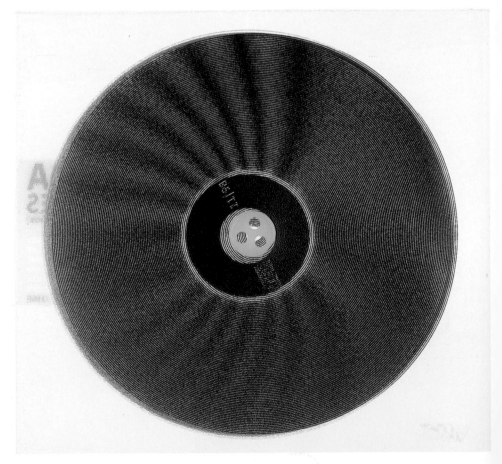

ltd.e
d98/
1000

ryoji ikeda
headphonics/lsds

plastic cd wallet &
cd with concentric
circular design
design: alorenz
mort aux vaches
1998

dan burke
illusion of safety

cd with wrap-around
sand-paper sleeve
design: rob meerman &
geert-jan hobijn
mort aux vaches
1997

lcd 11x

various/thurston moore
root

vacuum cleaner bag
packaging and cd
design: jon forss at
ekhornforss
lo recordings
1998

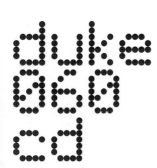

ripsnorter
slab

box, miscellaneous
contents & cd label
design: yacht
associates
hydrogen dukebox
1999

MOUSE ON MARS

wisc
478

mouse on mars
niun niggung

cd front & booklet
spreads
design: frieda luczak
at icon kommunikations-
design
zomba/domino (uk)/sonig
1999

a record is an object, a
thing, it's visual, and it
contains music.

christian marclay

interview in the wire

Bibliography

Barthes, Roland – *Image Music Text*
Fontana Press, 1977

Beard, Steve – *Logic Bomb*
Serpent's Tail, 1998

Eshun, Kodwo – *More Brilliant than the Sun:
Adventures in Sonic Fiction*
Quartet, 1998

Ferguson, Russell (Ed.) –
*Art and Film Since 1945:
Hall of Mirrors*
The Museum of Contemporary Art,
Los Angeles, 1996

Frith, Simon – *Performing Rites:
Evaluating Popular Music*
Oxford University Press, 1998

Gilroy, Paul – *The Black Atlantic*
Verso, 1993

Hickey, Dave – *Air Guitar:
Essays on Art & Democracy*
Art Issues Press, Los Angeles, 1997

James, Martin – *State of Bass:
Jungle: The Story so Far*
Boxtree, 1997

Klien, Naomi – *No Logo*
Flamingo, 2000

McRobbie, Angela – *In the Culture Society:
Art, Fashion and Popular Music*
Routledge, 1999

Muir, Robin – *Michael Cooper You are Here*
Schirmer/Mosel, 1999

Pesch, Martin and Weisbeck, Markus –
*Discstyle: The Graphic Arts of Electronic
Music and Club Culture*
(Preface by Ian Anderson)
Collins & Brown, 1999

Reid, Jamie and Savage, Jon –
*The Incomplete Works of Jamie Reid:
Up They Rise*
Faber and Faber, 1987

Reynolds, Simon – *Energy Flash*
Picador, 1998

Toop, David – *Exotica:
Fabricated Soundscapes in a Real World*
Serpent's Tail, 1999

Vaucher, Gee – *Crass Art and Other Pre
Post-Modernist Monsters*
AK Press, 1999

Wozencroft, Jon – *Touch & Fuse*
Touch, 1999

Magazines and articles

Bayley, Stephen – 'Hallelujah! Praise the
Brands', *Blueprint* No. 169, February 2000

Emigre No. 49, 'The Everything is for Sale
Issue'. Winter 1999

Eye 33, Vol. 9, Autumn 1999; various articles
on 'Pop music art' including long, insightful
essay by John O'Reilly

Garnett, Robert – Interview with Tim Gane of
Stereolab in *e2:4 the creamy issue,* 1998

Hoare, Philip – 'Icon to Icon',
The Independent on Sunday: Culture.
4 June 2000

Khazam, Rahma – Article on Christian
Marclay, *The Wire*, Issue 195, May 2000

Leahy, John – 'Art or commerce', article stating
the record industry view on sleeve design by
leading music business figure,
Creative Review, April 1999

Parkhurst, Roy – 'Tropisms. The Most
Beautiful Sound Next to Silence (A Personal
History of ECM)'. Found on the internet

+81, London Music Graphics issue, Vol. 71
Spring 2000

Poynor, Rick – 'Illustrate This' in *Frieze*,
Issue 49, November/December 1999

Rawsthorn, Alice – 'Pop Goes the Easel' in
*Wallpaper** 145, 1999

Relph-Knight, Lynda – Interview with Stefan
Sagmeister, *Design Week*, Vol. 15, No. 9,
March 2000

Reynolds, Simon – 'Wargasm: Military Imagery
in Popular Culture', *Frieze*, Issue 28, May 1996

Sabin, Roger – Interview with David Byrne in
Speak, Winter 1999

Toop, David – 'Sound Effects', review in
Bookforum, Volume 6, Issue 4, Winter 1999

Van Wissem, Jozef and Corrigan, Mariah –
Euro Vision' in *art/text*, No. 63,
November 1998/January 1999

White, Michael 'CD designers have a few
tricks up their sleeve', article in *The Globe
and Mail* (Canada), 29 April 2000

Young, Rob – 'Multi Media', article on Austrian
sleeve designers Abuse Industries, in *The Wire*,
Issue 180, February 1999

Discography

In recognition of the contribution made by various pieces of music to the creation of this book – and also because we like lists – the editors have provided a discography listing some of the music that provided the soundtrack to the production of *Sampler 2*.

2 Lone Swordsmen – *Stay Down*
Warp, 1998

Boredoms – *Super Are*
Birdman, 1999

Broadcast – *The Noise Made by People*
Warp, 2000

Cinematic Orchestra – *Motion*
Ninja Tune, 1999

Conjoint – *Earprints*
Source Records, 2000

Daniel Miller's *Happy Hour 22.11.00*
Private CD copy

Glen Brown and King Tubby –
Termination Dub 1973-79
Blood and Fire, 1997

Jean-Luc Godard – *Histoire(s) Du Cinema*
ECM, 2000

Miles Davis – *Get Up With It*
Columbia, 1974

Neu – *Neu 2*
Bootleg CD copy purchased on the internet

Nuno Canavarro – *Plux Quba*
Ama Romanta,1988

Raymond Scott – *Manhattan Research Inc.*
Basta, 2000

Richard Thomas – *Soggy Martyrs*
Lo, 1999

Roy Budd – *The Stone Killer*
Castle Music, 1999

Savath+Savalas – *Folk Songs for Trains, Trees and Honey*
Hefty, 2000

To Rococo Rot – *The Amateur View*
City Slang, 1999

The Intro Book Project team:

Writer: Adrian Shaughnessy
Designer: Julian House
Editors: Adrian Shaughnessy and Julian House
Business Affairs: Katy Richardson
Co-ordination: Debbie Glencross,
Jane Travers and Sarah Barlow
Creative interference: Mat Cook

Thanks

As before, numerous individuals gave help and guidance. Thanks are due to the following people: Cally Calloman at Antar; David Carr and Elaine Macintosh at Intro; Richard Chartier and Taylor Deupree at 12K; Laurent Fetis in Paris; Andrew Flack and Seb Marling at Blue Source; Jon Forss at EkhornForss; Jonas Grossmann at Source Records; Tom Hingston at Tom Hingston Studio; Geert-Jan Hobijn at Staalplaat; Seth Hodder, Daniel Miller and Paul Taylor at Mute; Mike Holdsworth at Matador; Trevor Jackson at Output; Jon Jeffrey at Farrow; Rune Kristoffersen at Rune Grammofon; Joel Lardner at Creative Union; Laurence King Publishing: Felicity Awdry, Simon Cowell, Laurence King, Jo Lightfoot, Janet Pilch and Laura Willis; Frieda Luczak and Eva Rusch at Icon; Rob Mitchell at Warp; Tony Morley at Leaf; Tim Owen at Jade Tree; Alan Parks and Juliet Sensicle at London; Bettina Richards at Thrill Jockey; Stefan Sagmeister at Sagmeister Inc.; Edward Shaughnessy; Andy Townsend at Pias; Hal Udell at Subtle Rukus; Rudy VanderLans at Emigre; John Walters at Eye; Mason Wells at North; Michael White in Vancouver; Jon Wozencroft at Touch; and finally Lewis Blackwell, whose original idea it was to create a book devoted to contemporary sleeve design – thanks to him for continued advice and support.

The following shops proved invaluable in locating hidden treasure. Frederic Sanchez, Paris; Other Music, New York; Rough Trade, Covent Garden, London; Selecta Disc, Berwick Street, London.

Dedicated to Daniel Miller and the Mute team, who consistently disregard the prevailing wisdom that decrees that sleeve design is no longer important.